Th. ~gy of
Conflict

The Psychology of Conflict

Mediating in a Diverse World

PAUL RANDOLPH

BLOOMSBURY

LONDON · OXFORD · NEW YORK · NEW DELHI · SYDNEY

Bloomsbury Continuum
An imprint of Bloomsbury Publishing Plc

50 Bedford Square
London
WC1B 3DP
UK

1385 Broadway
New York
NY 10018
USA

www.bloomsbury.com

First published 2016

British Library Cataloguing-in-Publication Data
A catalogue record for this book is available from the British Library.

Library of Congress Cataloguing-in-Publication data has been applied for.

ISBN: PB: 9781472922977
ePDF: 9781472922991
ePub: 9781472922984

2 4 6 8 10 9 7 5 3 1

Printed and bound in Great Britain by CPI Group (UK) Ltd, Croydon CR0 4YY

To find out more about our authors and books visit www.bloomsbury.com. Here you will find extracts, author interviews, details of forthcoming events and the option to sign up for our newsletters.

Dedicated to Daniel and Hannah

Contents

Note on the Author

Paul Randolph is a leading British mediator, trainer and writer whose approach adopts a subtle focus on the psychology of conflict and conflict management. He has mediated successfully in a wide variety of disputes, including commercial, family, workplace and professional negligence, with values of up to £130 million, and with as many as 16 parties. Paul's expertise in the psychology of disputes draws on his collaboration with the late Dr Freddie Strasser, the eminent psychotherapist with whom he designed the Mediation Skills course at the School of Psychotherapy and Counselling in Regent's University London. Since 1999 Paul has been Course Leader and has accredited over 1,000 mediators in the UK, Europe and Asia. Paul's previous book, *Mediation: A Psychological Insight into Conflict Resolution* (2004), was co-written with Dr Strasser. Paul is an accredited mediator (CEDR: June 1999, and SPC: May 2000) and barrister. He practises from Field Court Chambers in Gray's Inn, London. He is a member of the UK Bar Council ADR Committee and a Board member of the UK Civil Mediation Council. He is also a member of the Slynn Foundation, the European Mediation Network Initiative, the International Mediation Institute, the International Bar Association (IBA), BIMA (Belief in Mediation and Arbitration), and until recently was on the Professional Standards Committee of the College of Mediators. He is an External Examiner for Mediation on the LLM at Kingston

University. Paul Randolph's emphasis on the psychological aspects of mediation and conflict resolution has received wide acclaim with British and international audiences. He has given presentations and masterclasses on the application of psychology in mediation and in conflict management to professional and official organizations in the UK and throughout central and eastern Europe, as well as in China, India, South Africa, North and South America, Singapore, Russia, Turkey and Jordan.

Acknowledgements

A large number of people contributed, directly or indirectly, to the writing of this book. I am indebted first to my wife, Karen, who served throughout as my sounding board for matters of style and expression. As a gentle critic of my old-fashioned – if not Dickensian – style of writing, she helped to chaperone me away from the archaic legalese to a more contemporary model of prose. Her patience and understanding as I worked through holidays, weekends and nights to realize my publisher's deadline was an immeasurable encouragement and invaluable support.

Insofar as content is concerned, this book would not have been written without the influence and stimulus of Karen Weixel-Dixon, a dear friend and colleague tutor on the Mediation Skills course at Regent's University London. Karen was present in 1998 at the outset of the course, assisting and guiding Dr Freddie Strasser and me in the planning and implementation stages of the programme – a programme that was to be rolled out so successfully over the years since then. Of course, it was the inspirational inducement of Dr Freddie Strasser that first brought me into the world of psychotherapy and his uniquely charismatic leadership of the mediation course provided me with my first motivation towards existential psychology. Without Freddie, neither the course nor I would be where we are now, for it was through him that I found myself propelled into an evangelistic and stimulating second career. It was Karen Weixel-Dixon, however, who, as a tutor on the course virtually throughout the period of its existence, helped me to gain a deeper understanding of some of the existential and phenomenological concepts so fervently advocated by Freddie. Her guidance on the chapter on Existentialism was very warmly appreciated.

Following closely behind Karen Weixel-Dixon in terms of the contribution to my education in existential psychotherapy and psychology are the other tutors on the Mediation Skills course at RUL. Monica Hanaway and Diana Mitchell have, over a long period as tutors on the course, helped to refine my lectures on 'Why Psychology?'. It was during this period that they assisted me in modifying and honing my lawyer's perspective on psychology in conflict. More recently, Spenser Hilliard, a fellow tutor and a colleague from my Chambers in Lamb Building and Field Court, managed, through our frequent debates and discussions on training trips abroad, to shape – and correct – some of my interpretations and standpoints. Sanja Oakley and Greg Madison, and other tutors too numerous to mention, were all beneficial contributors along the path to my edification and to the writing of this book.

Finally, but by no means the least influential, are my children, Daniel and Hannah. Their faces were constant mental images that were with me while writing the book, and it is they to whom this book was aimed and is now dedicated. Daniel, with his enviable talent for figures and mathematical hypotheses, may be less likely to encounter the need for a psychotherapeutic approach to conflict; nevertheless, his balanced and pragmatic outlook on life is well reflected in the messages in this book. Hannah is a 'natural-born mediator'. Trained and accredited by the best (at RUL, of course!), her passion for mediation is heart-warming; and is equally matched by her aptitude and astounding skill for the process. It would be a pleasing thought if this book were to form part of a mediation legacy that is left to her.

I would have liked this book to stand as some form of testament to Freddie, and also to my late mother, who was Freddie's sister and whose atmospheric paintings enrich the covers of both this and our previous book. I am deeply indebted to Freddie for drawing me into this fascinating world of psychology, and my mother was so gratified that we were able to work together in this field. Yet this book could never aspire to the quality required to be a fitting tribute to him. I just hope he would have regarded it as 'good enough'.

Foreword by
Archbishop Desmond Tutu

While humankind has made fantastic technological, engineering, scientific and medical advances over the past few centuries, we have failed to match this progress when it comes to managing conflict.

We inhabit a world once considered vast – recently reduced through our connectivity to what we term a global village. But when relationships in the village sour, we all too often slip backwards into selfishness, anger and violence. We seem all too ready to subvert our innate goodness, our compassion, our sensibility, sensitivity and the love with which we were born. Injustice, aggression, oppression and inequity are the consequences of this foolishness.

Why do we lapse into conflict so easily? Why does it seem so difficult to turn the other cheek, to apologise when we have done wrong, to reconcile, to forgive?

In the pages to follow, Paul Randolph seeks to provide answers to this conundrum through a succinct analysis of some of the philosophies of Existentialism. The thrust of his argument is that existential concepts enhance our appreciation of some of the fundamental human characteristics that we all share – the 'existential givens' – irrespective of how we look, where we come from, our religious beliefs, cultural practices and monetary wealth.

We may inhabit different continents and live very different lifestyles, but – in a very real sense – we are all members of one family, the human family. I call it God's family. We all love, laugh, cry and bleed. Whoever we are and wherever we live, we all share the challenges of managing time, temporality, transiency and our own mortality – and we all share the affliction of having to face uncertainty. We all create values for ourselves, and construct our self-esteem, maintaining an image of our self-worth. These 'existential givens' mould the coping mechanisms we adopt when facing our challenges.

Randolph draws on the concepts proposed by leading existentialists such as Kierkegaard, Heidegger, Husserl and Sartre, to demonstrate how we create inter-personal relationships to cope with uncertainty and to provide us with aspirations and meanings in life.

Most importantly, we learn of the impact of emotions upon reason; that when we are in conflict we are driven, not by logic but by overwhelming emotions. These emotions are triggered by our self-esteem, our values, perceptions, assumptions and biases. We get angry when the things we care about most – our values – are attacked, and when our self-image is jeopardised.

In the first chapter of the book Randolph draws attention to complementarities between existential concepts and the South African philosophy of *Ubuntu*. While *Ubuntu* emphasizes our common humanity, connectedness and interdependence, existentialists grapple with the phenomena of how we exist in the world in space and in time, and how we relate to others. Both philosophies identify our need to embrace inter-personal relationships as an existential given. As *Ubuntu* simply states it: we are made for each other.

Randolph demonstrates how Heidegger's concept of our existence in relation to others and the rest of the world mirrors the principles of *Ubuntu*. Heidegger's view of our inter-connectedness was based, like that of Sartre, upon the belief that we do not exist in isolation. Even when isolated, we are isolated *from* others. Heidegger was, incidentally, a Catholic greatly influenced by the writings of Saint Augustine. And Kierkegaard, often regarded as the father of existentialism, was deeply religious and illustrated the concept of freedom of choice with the biblical accounts of Adam and Eve, and the 'paradox of objective truth', the story of Abraham and Isaac.

Through juxtaposing philosophical theory with its very practical application in the field of human conflict, Randolph succeeds in persuading us that an understanding of the psychology of human behaviour is an invaluable tool for managing conflict: for nurturing harmony and sustainability in the human family.

Desmond M. Tutu

Cape Town, 2015

Introduction

I am not a psychologist. I am a barrister who spent 35 years as an ardent litigator – until I 'saw the light' and discovered another and better way of resolving conflict. Since 1997, when the Mediation Skills course at Regent's University London (then Regent's College) was first planned and created, I have been surrounded by psychotherapists steeped in existential philosophies. Through the Alternative Dispute Resolution Faculty of psychotherapist tutors at Regent's University London, and primarily under the late and great Dr Freddie Strasser, I became increasingly aware of the powerful benefits that existentialist theories can bring to all aspects of conflict management. This led to Dr Strasser and me writing our book, *Mediation: A Psychological Insight into Conflict Resolution*, which was published by Continuum in 2004. At that time, my knowledge and understanding of existentialism were in their early stages of development. Since then and over the past 11 years, the ADR courses at RUL have continued to flourish, and, in my capacity as Course Leader teaching on the courses and interacting with the psychotherapist tutors, my understanding has deepened and the knowledge has broadened.

This book, however, is not proposed as an academic discourse on existentialism, but rather as a lawyer's perspective upon some of the more practical applications of the philosophy, as encountered by many who have to deal with conflict. It was born initially out of a desire to update and revise the earlier book; but it very quickly became apparent that much more needed to be said than might be covered simply by a revised edition. This book is therefore aimed not only at the accredited and professional mediator, but also at all those involved in conflict, whether engaged with conflict avoidance, conflict management or conflict resolution. As stated in Chapter 2, the term 'mediator' is used throughout the work to encompass lawyers, diplomats, politicians and national leaders, HR executives, police officers, hostage negotiators and any others who are called upon to assist or intervene in, negotiate or manage conflict. It is hoped that the contents of these chapters will be of useful application in commercial, international, community, family and workplace disputes, as well as simply in social and domestic quarrels.

The book commences with a chapter on Existentialism, seeking to demonstrate how existential philosophies are relevant to an understanding of human behaviour in conflicts generally, as well as in mediation and other dispute resolution processes. In particular, it looks at some of the philosophies of Kierkegaard, Heidegger, Husserl, Merleau-Ponty and Sartre, and examines how they translate into a practical application of existential psychology to the benefit of all those involved in negotiation, mediation and ADR generally. It goes on to outline some of the shared existential 'givens' (such as Emotions, Time and Temporality, Uncertainty, Self-Esteem and others) that are dealt with in greater detail in the ensuing chapters.

Chapter 2 looks at the role of the mediator from a psychological perspective, identifying a mediator's principal aim as one of securing an attitude shift on the part of those in dispute. This, it is shown, cannot be achieved through the application of logical persuasion, and the chapter concludes by outlining some of the 'person-centred' communication skills, as indicated by Carl Rogers, the twentieth-century American psychologist, required to fulfil the mediator's role. Chapter 3 looks at the influence of emotions in conflict and in conflict-resolution processes. It identifies how emotions are the driving force that appear to overwhelm reason in dispute situations, and provides explanations for the seemingly 'irrational' behaviour of those caught up in conflict. Chapter 4 examines the role of self-esteem as one of the most powerful motivating factors in a conflict: it considers how our 'self-concept' translates into nearly all our actions and decisions, governing our behaviour and precipitating a variety of behavioural strategies in conflict situations. It identifies our craving for approval, our constant need for control, and highlights some of the coping mechanisms that we adopt in order to address the uncertainty and transiency of our daily existence. Chapter 5 deals with Values, Sedimentations and Polarities, examining the creation of our value systems, how values are linked to self-esteem and emotions, and how they can become 'sedimented' – so rigid as to be impervious to rationalization. The chapter reveals how values in turn create polarities, and how a mediator can work effectively with polarities and sedimented values so as to secure an attitude shift. Chapter 6 looks at our universal need to be heard and how we create interpersonal relationships, as a demonstration of our shared existential givens, and an example of our coping mechanisms in response to the existential concepts of uncertainty, time and temporality. Chapter 7 describes the ways in which perceptions, assumptions and biases can be important driving forces in conflicts.

It considers the perception shift as a modification of the disputant's aims and objectives from the 'ideal' to the 'good enough'.

Chapter 8, 'The Practical Application of Psychology to Mediation', studies some of the typical problems that arise during the conduct of a mediation, and proposes some psychologically informed methods of dealing with and overcoming them. It examines the party's reluctance to mediate, the pitfalls that can be encountered in joint sessions, the setting and enforcement of 'ground rules' and the complications that might arise in concluding the settlement agreement. Chapter 9 surveys some varying models of mediation and the psychological challenges that they can generate. It looks at the Harvard model of 'shuttle' commercial mediation, family, community, and workplace mediation, as well as the restorative justice model, and considers the respective relevance of existential philosophies and psychology to each of these. The book concludes in Chapter 10 with speculation as to the future of mediation. It scrutinizes the manner in which mediation is promoted, and explores some of the issues surrounding the issue of compulsion to mediate. The debate continues as to the benefits of training more mediators, and the chapter looks at this issue together with the differing styles of mediation adopted by mediators, such as 'Narrative', 'Transformative', 'Evaluative', and 'Facilitative': these styles are briefly considered from a psychological viewpoint. The future of mediation in cross-cultural dispute resolution is also discussed, identifying the relevance and assistance that existential philosophies and psychology can provide when applied in such disputes. The chapter closes with a brief overview of regulation, and the European Directive and various Codes of Conduct for mediators.

1

Existentialism – Its Relevance to Conflict and Dispute Resolution

Conflict takes place in a diverse world – a world of ethnic, national, geographical, cultural, economic, social, religious and legal differences. This presents a daunting challenge to those who deal with conflict, whether in its avoidance, management or resolution. Yet all human beings, irrespective of their birthplace or the environment in which they were nurtured, share a vast majority of identical characteristics and qualities. It is a basic premise underpinning this book that these characteristics, referred to as 'existential givens', represent the many commonalities shared by all in human existence. They demonstrate the extent to which we are all alike, and are therefore a key to understanding our behaviour in conflict. Consequently, if we are to be effective in dealing with conflict, we will benefit from a true appreciation of these universal 'givens' of the human condition.

Appreciating that those in dispute share a substantial number of the same human characteristics and qualities can be helpful and reassuring to mediators and those involved in managing or resolving conflict. Mediators may find that a clear insight into these shared attributes, and a comprehension of the behavioural strategies adopted by those in dispute, are invaluable. Existentialist philosophies provide just such insights: they furnish an essential comprehension of the many commonalities shared by all in human existence. In this way, the existentialists shine a revelatory light upon the myriad issues that confront all those who have to deal with conflict on a regular basis.

Existentialist Philosophy

To some, the word 'existentialism' will conjure up a picture of smoke-filled Parisian cafés, with intellectuals discussing death, nihilism and Nietzsche. To others, it will be a forbidding and unapproachable concept, shrouded in perplexing mystique.

It is unfortunate that much of the writing by – as well as about – existentialists is impenetrable. It is frequently written in elusive and obscure language, and the literature of the great exponents of this philosophical model tends to deter all but the committed academic. Some of the obscurity stems from the difficulties of definition of the philosophy itself and of its constituent parts. The label 'existentialism' was unknown to those such as Nietzsche and Kierkegaard, the latter now described by many as the founder of the philosophy. Baroness Mary Warnock stated in *Existentialism*:

> 'Existentialism', like 'Rationalism' or 'Empiricism' is a label that may mislead the unwary. It does not designate a system or a school; there are some philosophers who might be described as

Existentialists but who would reject the title; others who might be surprised to be so described ... We may be content to use the term 'Existentialism' to cover a kind of philosophical activity which flourished on the Continent especially in the 1940's and 1950's, which can be shown to have certain common interests, common ancestry, and common presuppositions ...

(1970: 1)

For the purposes of this book, it matters little whether existentialism is a philosophical activity, a cultural movement, or simply a mode of thinking. The important aspect is that its philosophical concepts answer many puzzling questions that litigators, mediators, diplomats and negotiators often have when confronting those in dispute. All those with the task of managing and resolving disputes, as well as those friends and colleagues on the periphery or sitting on the sidelines, will at some point find themselves asking the same rhetorical questions: 'Why do sensible, intelligent, rational people appear to act so irrationally? Why do commercial business people behave so uncommercially and in such a child-like manner when in conflict? What is it that so quickly drives people into intense and bitter disputes?' Existential philosophies can provide answers.

When unravelled, deconstructed, interpreted and laid bare to their most unassuming concepts, existential philosophies constitute an extremely practical and down-to-earth approach to everyday human behaviour, and help provide some explanation in response to many of these questions. They present observations of many of the characteristics of our human condition that are particularly relevant and applicable in conflict situations. The concept of shared existential givens will demonstrate that all those in conflict face similar problems and challenges: for example, they must all engage with time and temporality; they all need to cope with transiency; they all experience the anxiety and distress of uncertainty; they are each driven by self-esteem; they together have a need for interpersonal relationships; they each create values by which they feel they must live; and they all enjoy freedom of choice, which they believe must nevertheless be exercised with responsibility. It is how each of us responds to these shared givens – our coping mechanisms – that creates the differences in our human existence. Understanding these commonalities and responses can help to enlighten us with explanations for some of the conundrums of human behaviour in conflict: why nations are led to the brink of war by the intransigent stances adopted by their leaders; why cost-conscious, commercially oriented, risk-averse, business-like chief executives drag their companies into futile protracted litigation, when it would be commercially more sensible swiftly to resolve their dispute; why family members are willing to squander their inheritance in prolonged lawsuits, when the 'pot' over which they are arguing diminishes in size with each day that they remain in dispute; why employees, neighbours and friends are all prepared to blight their daily lives with – at least to the observer – trivial and insignificant disagreements; and why they allow them to escalate into fiercely intense confrontations. Later chapters in this book will demonstrate, for example, how emotions and self-esteem respectively inform and govern our behaviour; and how our values and rigid sedimentations may limit our apparent freedom to choose the way we respond to and deal with conflict.

It is through an examination of human existence – how we exist in the world and how we interrelate with and respond to others – that we can acquire an understanding of the various behavioural strategies that we adopt in such conflict situations. By a better understanding, first of ourselves, and then of others, we are able to facilitate a greater comprehension of the coping mechanisms applied by those in conflict. It is these human traits which, though shared, can nevertheless often create psychological blockages to the resolution of disputes. By identifying and recognizing them, the mediator can consider how best to work *with* them, so as to bring about a material change in attitude and secure that all-important shift in perceptions and expectations as to the outcome of the dispute.

The Existentialists

A theme that preoccupies many existentialists and which they share in common is that we are all 'thrown into' an uncertain world, and the manner in which we cope with that predicament involves an analysis of 'the self', freedom of choice, truth and objectivity, uncertainty, meaning and absurdity. These are all themes regularly encountered by mediators and those dealing with conflict. They may go unrecognized as existential ideas, but are all issues with which most of those in dispute will in some way struggle at some point, whether knowingly or unknowingly. It may be helpful briefly to examine some of the views of the principal protagonists of existentialist thought in order to appreciate the nature and extent of their relevance to mediation.

Søren Kierkegaard (1813–55)

Søren Kierkegaard foreshadowed the twentieth-century existentialists and is often described as 'the father of modern existentialism' (see for example Mick Cooper, 2003: 7). Kierkegaard's writings are frequently obscure, difficult and sometimes quite impenetrable. However, in two of his seminal works he chooses biblical examples to assist him in his analyses of some these themes referred to above. In *The Concept of Anxiety* (or 'angst') (1844) he seeks to propose an explanation for the manner in which, in the biblical account, Adam exercises his freedom to choose: what is it that makes him eat the apple in the face of a contrary commandment from God? According to the Bible, prior to God's prohibition Adam would not have had any concept of 'polarities' such as good and evil or right and wrong. He would have had no real comprehension of 'certain death', with which he was threatened should he transgress: for he had not at that stage experienced death in any form, nor had been given any reason to contemplate it. Yet he exercises his freedom to choose with a huge leap into the unknown, and in utter contravention of God's directive. Kierkegaard explains this by proposing that God's commandment awakens an 'anxiety' in Adam resulting from the revelation of an infinite number of *possibilities*. To Kierkegaard, anxiety is fundamental proof of our existence as individuals: it 'takes us out of our comfort zone', while demonstrating that we are free – free to choose. 'The relationship of freedom to guilt is anxiety, because freedom and guilt remain possibilities' (1844: 97). Kierkegaard compares anxiety to a 'dizziness' – the dizziness of freedom similar to that experienced when standing on the edge of an abyss staring into an expanse of endless possibilities. In this way, anxiety is more acute and less manageable than pure fear. Fear is always 'intentional' and finite, in the sense of being directed at, and explicitly referable to, some object. We are never fearful in a vacuum, but always afraid of *something*. Anxiety, on the other hand, is nebulous and imprecise and not directed at anything specific.

It is just such anxiety that a mediator may see displayed by the parties to a dispute as they face a variety of difficult choices and possibilities. It may be of little comfort to the parties to be told by the mediator that their anxieties demonstrate that they are individuals; yet by understanding the nature and provenance of this *angst* and its relation to the realm of possibilities, the mediator may be better able to assist the parties in analysing their options. By helping parties in conflict explore the choices available to them, the mediator fulfils a crucial and important role: 'You have the option of choosing A or B: let us consider what are the consequences of choosing A and rejecting B. Now let us consider what might happen on the other hand if you accept B and reject A.' This analytical process at the same time underlines the essential component of the parties' freedom to choose.

A possibly greater contribution by Kierkegaard to the philosophy of conflict, insofar as it serves the mediator's purpose, is his proposition of the paradoxical relationship between truth, objectivity and subjectivity. The absence of any objective truth as perceived by parties to a dispute is a phenomenon well known to all mediators and those involved in conflict, and is further demonstrated in the following chapter. The 'search for truth' underpins most legal jurisdictions, and is an essential driver in nearly all disputes. The moral philosophy of both Nietzsche and Kierkegaard has a common approach that 'ultimately stems from a theory of the truth' (Warnock: 13). Kierkegaard wrote in his work *Concluding Unscientific Postscript* (1846: 183): 'The paradoxical character of the truth is its objective uncertainty.' For Kierkegaard the real truth is achieved only through a 'passionate' commitment to existence. There is no such concept as 'objective truth': no truth is universal, but, rather, truth is what is true for the individual. As Polonius advises Laertes in Shakespeare's *Hamlet*:

> This above all: to thine own self be true,
> And it must follow, as the night the day,
> Thou canst not then be false to any man.
>
> (*Hamlet*, Act I, Scene iii)

So it is for litigants and those involved in disputes: each party fervently believes their position to be the only objective and universal truth. They are driven in the belief that they are being true to themselves, and that a judge, arbitrator, mediator or other conflict resolver will eventually agree with their objective truth.

In *Fear and Trembling* (1843), Kierkegaard uses another biblical story, this time of Abraham and Isaac, to demonstrate the paradox between moral and ethical principles on the one hand and inexplicable faith on the other. What was it that drove Abraham to break the highest universal ethical and moral code in an attempt to kill his son? An appreciation of the answer to this question may help a mediator when faced with parties apparently exercising their choices in equally 'absurd' ways. To any 'objective' observer, Abraham's actions are incomprehensible and seemingly insane. No amount of logical explanation can serve to render them comprehensible to others. To Abraham, however, it was his passionate commitment to existing as an authentic individual that provided him with a truth that was true for him and him alone. Subjective truths are incapable of objective elucidation. Only those standing precisely in Abraham's shoes, seeing the world as he saw it – his 'worldview' – experiencing the same passionate faith as he, can possibly have any appreciation of the drivers that motivated his behaviour. A mediator will often strive to gain a comprehensive understanding of the behaviour of parties in dispute, in order effectively to empathize. But Kierkegaard demonstrates through the biblical example of Abraham that it may *never* be possible *completely* to understand, nor able *fully* to fathom, the choices the parties make. The mediator may therefore need simply to adopt an attitude of non-judgmental acceptance – accepting the parties' position at their own assessment, without challenge or question, however difficult this counter-intuitive stance may be (see further Chapter 6). Similarly, through an appreciation of Kierkegaard's proposition, the mediator can help the parties by encouraging them to accept the fact that they also may never be able wholly to comprehend the actions of the other. The realization that there is no such thing as absolute objective truth may assist in delivering that vital change of attitude necessary for resolution.

Edmund Husserl (1859–1938)

Edmund Husserl, a German professor of philosophy, further contributed to the analysis of existence through the philosophical school of 'phenomenology'. This can be translated literally from the Greek as 'the study of appearances'. By his process of phenomenology, Husserl sought to 'make sense' of the apparent nature of experiences – as they appeared and were experienced by the person from a 'first-person' perspective. Objects were not objects in themselves, but only objects in terms of their appearance, their use, their function and their purpose. He deflected the significance of objective facts, and focused upon 'subjective experiences'. All existence is merely a subjective interpretation of being, and it is not feasible to provide an objective rationalization. This involves a 'suspending, or bracketing', of assumptions about the physical existence of objects while concentrating on the subjective experiences of them. By stripping away all ordinary and natural assumptions about things, we come closer to being able to see them as they really exist. Thus a phenomenological approach enables us to understand the interpretations placed upon others by those in dispute. It enables the mediator better to appreciate the meanings attributed to a party's own position and to that of the other party.

Mediators are urged and taught to 'bracket' their own assumptions. They are nevertheless made to realize that it is never possible entirely to put our assumptions and prejudices to one side: they will always be present, and the importance lies in being sufficiently self-aware so as not to allow our biases to interfere with our understandings. If and when the parties in dispute are able to recognize and acknowledge their own assumptions, prejudices and biases, the bitterness of the conflict inevitably diminishes. It is for this reason that the students of mediation are taught not merely to elicit facts from the parties, but to focus upon the parties' subjective *experience* of those facts. It is not the ostensible appearance of those facts that matters, but the manner in which they are experienced subjectively.

Parties in the dispute will experience the facts, and will view the other party, from a wholly subjective perspective. This perspective will be in stark contrast to that of the opposing party – and possibly may also be far removed from that of the mediator. For example, a party may see the other not as the individual that he or she is, but as the scoundrel who perpetrated an injustice. On the other hand, they may genuinely believe they see their opponent's point of view from a subjective perspective – 'we do understand where they are coming from' – when in fact they cannot do so, nor can they be expected to do so. Further, a party may not even wish truly to comprehend the position of the other, as it may involve completely altering their perception of themselves and of the dispute, and may possibly necessitate a modification of their entire worldview. Yet again, for the mediator these factors demand a phenomenological approach: they will involve an element of empathy – stepping into the shoes of a party so as to experience as far as is possible the facts from a 'first-person' perspective. We all constantly interpret facts: it is therefore vital for a mediator to gain a phenomenological understanding of how parties in dispute interpret the facts to themselves. Without such an appreciation, the mediator will find it difficult to assist parties in achieving a 'perception shift'.

Martin Heidegger (1889–1976)

Martin Heidegger, a German philosopher, made a further and significant contribution to the existential school of thought. Indeed, Warnock (1970: 46) considered Heidegger to be the 'first true Existentialist'. One of his central themes is an exploration of the nature of 'Being'. In his seminal work *Sein und Zeit* (Being and Time), written in 1927, he approached the essence of being in the term '*Dasein*', literally translated meaning 'being there'. It is the word 'there' that is important, for it denotes Heidegger's view of our existence as it is in relation to others and to the rest of the world. For it is not only 'being-in-the-world' but also 'being-in-the world-with-others' that is important. (The hyphens reflect Heidegger's view of the interconnected nature of the concept.) We do not exist in isolation – and even when isolated, we are isolated *from others*. Thus the concept of relatedness, and the notion of our creation of interpersonal relationships, is given wings.

> Indeed, this relationship starts from birth, in that as soon as we are 'thrown' into the world, we are immediately confronted with others. As such Heidegger demonstrates that humans have an inescapable relationship with one another ... Our natural state is the state of communion with people who participate in one another's private world. This is an interdependent world and fundamentally a world of togetherness.
>
> (Strasser and Strasser, 1997: 23)

Our relationship and relatedness to others is never more sharply in focus than when we are in dispute or conflict with others. It is the manner in which we choose to exist with others that leads to conflict, and also ultimately governs the possibilities of achieving the resolution of conflict.

Heidegger goes on to consider the relationship between people and the world as one of 'care and concern' (in German, '*Sorge*'). This is not an ethical or benevolent notion of 'care': the concern involves man's existence against the background of time and temporality (*Zeitlichkeit*). An awareness of future time is an important aspect of Heidegger's concept of existence. We are thrown into a world over which we have little or no control; the past, present and future are all inextricably woven together; but for Heidegger, it is the future that holds the greatest 'possibilities'. 'Everything begins with the future' (Heidegger, 2001: 159). Future time is determinative of the present, and human behaviour is *purposeful* rather than *caused*. This self-awareness (*Gewissheit*) as described by Heidegger, which acknowledges human existence as a synthesis of the facts of the past, the instant present and the possibilities of the future, renders the human being more 'authentic' and more readily able to make 'conscientious' choices.

For existentialists, time is not linear and so is not to be measured; but, rather, it is a matter of how it is experienced. This contribution may again be seen as being of relevance to the mediator. Parties in dispute find their existence in the world wholly dependent upon their context in time: it is how they experience and engage with time that is important to the disputant and also to the mediator. The loss of time, whether past, present or future, is often at the heart of a dispute. Time can never be recovered; so 'wasting time', 'making up for lost time', 'productive use of time', 'gaining time' are all common concerns manifested by parties in conflict. A party's obsessive analysis of things past may need to be viewed in the light of the realization that past time cannot be retrieved; and a preoccupation with the future may render the party's experience of the present utterly meaningless. So a consideration of what the future may hold, while bringing with it an abundance of uncertainty, can also create a wealth of possibilities and opportunities. Such an approach is likely to be considered constructive to a mediator, and more in keeping with the mediator's role of urging parties to 'move forward' and look to the future, rather than dwelling obsessively in the past.

Heidegger's proposals of time and temporality may thus helpfully inform the mediator. To Heidegger, the past, present and future are not distinct entities: all three are present in every moment of existence; and each moment becomes the past and the future in the blink of an eye. In other words, our existence cuts across time. Mary Warnock interprets Heidegger's proposition in this way (1970):

> [Heidegger] argues that the future is not a mere set of instants, each of which is about to become the present instant, but rather that the existence of future time actually determines, and is logically prior to present time ... the present, for the authentic human being, is a synthesis of past and future, since he knows what he was, and what he resolves to be, and it is this upon which he is concentrated.
>
> (1970: 63)

The concept of an 'authentic' human being, as set out in *Sein und Zeit* (Being and Time), is a further element of Heidegger's philosophy that may be of relevance to a mediator. Heidegger's approach to being authentic and living authentically involves a thorough and prerequisite level of self-awareness, particularly in relation to our existence in time. It is vital to be able to open ourselves up and through this to appreciate our unique and individual qualities, to recognize the possibilities that are available to us, and to accept the responsibilities that this creates. This will, of course, apply directly not only to the parties in conflict in the mediation, but equally to the mediator himself. For the mediator to be effective, he must maintain a level of self-awareness throughout his involvement with the parties. Again, Mary Warnock puts it succinctly:

> [Heidegger] is suggesting that if a human being is aware of himself as a being based on the facts of his past and also as projected towards the future which he chooses, then he will take full responsibility for his life, and he will recognise that his choices are his own, not dictated any longer by what people in general do or expect.
>
> (1970: 64)

In other words, the choices a party makes 'in the present' will be closely interrelated with the past and the future. This applies equally from a mediator's perspective, in relation to the choices that are available as to how the mediation is to be conducted.

But in order fully to understand Heidegger's view of *authenticity*, it must be both compared and contrasted with his outlook on *in*-authenticity. Although he sought not to make a judgment as to which mode of being was good and which was bad, Heidegger argued that to be inauthentic or to live inauthentically was to live in a way that failed properly to confront our true self, essentially in relation to time and temporality, and ultimately in relation to death. He described the 'facticity' of our existence as a plain and undeniable *fact* of our 'being-in-the-world', and suggested that we have been 'thrown' into the world (the concept he described as *Geworfenheit*), without our choosing and without any determination of what or who we are. Against this, it is necessary to realise our *finitude* or limitations, and that we are always in a trajectory towards death. Failure to appreciate this leads to inauthenticity. In this way a new emphasis is placed upon the commitment involved in every decision made, when viewed in the light of impending finality or death.

This does not mean that parties in dispute must always be urged by the mediator to contemplate death. But it does mean that we may all benefit from being reminded or being conscious of the finite nature of our predicament and of the choices open to us. This may then affect the way we choose and influence the exercise of our freedom to do so. To take a commonplace example, if an article is on display for sale accompanied by a sign stating: 'All transactions are deemed full and final – no returns, exchanges or refunds will be permitted', the decision and choice over whether or not to make the purchase will inevitably become more focused.

> With the anxious awareness of my own death, my decisions and commitments are made with a renewed sense of urgency and focus, with the recognition that the stand I take on my situation contributes to the realisation of the kind of person I am, and that I alone am responsible for the coherence, integrity, and direction of my life.
>
> (Aho, 2014: 97)

An authentic acceptance of ourselves and our limitations will lead to the adoption of a different attitude towards the future, as well as the past and the present. It also brings with it the all-important concept of responsibility – taking responsibility for, and appreciating the possible future consequences of, our actions and choices.

Heidegger's approach to authenticity involved a recognition of being authentic *in relation to others*. For Heidegger, as with many existentialists, existence is fundamentally relational: we are always in relation to others, whether by proximity or by separational distance. *Dasein* is about 'being-in-the-world', an inseparable relationship with location and with others. The person in conflict who shirks the need to take responsibility for the future choices he makes, as it affects others, will fall within Heidegger's description of inauthenticity. Such a person is unable to adopt a proper level of self-awareness, cannot be open with himself and fails to understand the concepts of 'finitude'. This link to being responsible and taking proper responsibility for the choices we make is important to the mediator, as it is to all those bound up in conflict.

Maurice Merleau-Ponty (1907–61)

The French philosopher Maurice Merleau-Ponty, greatly influenced by Husserl and Heidegger, approached existence as a matter of *bodily* perception, and sought to explain that consciousness lives through the body. The embodied nature of our existence is bound up in our mental experiences, and our understanding of the world is in fact 'embodied'. The mediator will recognize phrases such as 'gut reaction', a 'feeling in the pit of the stomach', 'a weight off the shoulders', 'heart-felt sentiments', 'hair-raising experience', 'tremble with fear', 'arms-length decisions', as possible evidence of a party's corporeal experience of a dispute.

It may also be interesting to note the 'embodiment' entailed by fear and anxiety. Someone experiencing fear, as for example when speaking in public, may suffer from bodily sensations such as 'butterflies in the stomach', a drying of the mouth, undue perspiration, a 'pounding' of the heart, uncontrollable blushing and, on occasions, trembling of the limbs. This view of embodiment reflected and to some extent complemented the hypothesis of subjectivity, as proposed by both Kierkegaard and Heidegger. The perspective that comes from detached objectivity is rejected in favour of that which emanates from 'first-person' activities and embodied experiences. The body is not merely a 'passive object' that reacts to outside influences, or external stimuli, but one that actively generates its own consciousness through its perceiving of the outside world.

Merleau-Ponty's analysis of perceptions involves a particular view that science and empirical analysis are not adequate paradigms or models for understanding human existence. This is outlined in the preface to his work *Phenomenology of Perception* (1945), in which he emphasizes the fact that science 'is built upon the world as directly experienced':

> Science has not, and never will have by its nature, the same significance *qua* form of being as the world which we perceive, for the simple reason that it is a rationale or explanation of that world. I am not 'a living creature', not even a 'man', not again even 'consciousness' endowed with all the characteristics which zoology, social anatomy, or inductive psychology recognise in these various products of the natural or historical process – I am the absolute source, my existence does not stem from my antecedents, from my physical and social environment; instead it moves outwards towards them and sustains them …
>
> Merleau-Ponty's Preface, p. viii, cited by Warnock (1970: 75)

Merleau-Ponty thus proposed that empirical knowledge is preceded by individual perceptions. He was concerned to demonstrate the relationship between consciousness and the 'outside' world. This is important for the mediator, for an understanding of a party's perceptions and how they connect with the remainder of the perceived world will be of significant value in any attempt at reality-testing or challenging a party's perceptions.

Further elements of Merleau-Ponty's approach to existence are his concepts of time and temporality, and freedom. He deals with these topics in the final two chapters of *Phenomenology of Perception*. Though less central than his propositions on perceptions and embodiment, they are nevertheless of relevance to the mediator. Warnock describes them in this way: 'Thus both consciousness of self, in a minimal sense, and consciousness of time, are absolutely essential to our existence in the world as beings who can perceive and who can act' (1970: 88).

Merleau-Ponty's proposition is that, yet again, time and temporality are to be viewed in a wholly subjective manner: neither the past nor the future can exist 'now', and consequently neither is capable of scientific observation or analysis. Parties in dispute may frequently need reminding of this by the mediator: that both the past and the future exist only in their perceptions. Memories of past events are notorious for their distortion; a party's recollection of historic occurrences and happenings are likely to be grossly inaccurate. The constant and fixated exploration of past events may therefore be futile. Similarly with the future: those in conflict may have an overly optimistic or unduly pessimistic perception of future possibilities. Litigants often cherish a naïve conviction that if only they win their case, 'everything in the garden will be rosy'. Conversely, they may feel hopelessly destined to failure, so that whatever they do, it will be wrong. Undue speculation as to the future in these circumstances is likely to be fruitless.

Merleau-Ponty also shone a light on the ambiguity of freedom. To exist in the world is at once to be totally free, and yet at the same time to be limited by our perceptions of obstacles to that freedom. The very notion of a perceived obstacle underlines the fact that we are free; for without obstacles there would be no freedom. The limits to freedom are a consequence of our being in a world made up of social, physical and economic limitations. One obstacle to complete freedom is our acquisition and possession of sedimented experiences: these are assumptions, habits, stances and positions that we take for granted and to which we give little real thought. We may, for example, have an assumption that tidiness means efficiency; consequently when we are confronted with untidiness, our freedom to make unbiased choices about an untidy person or a 'messy' office are severely restricted. We shall see (in Chapter 5) how these rigid sedimentations can be impervious to rationalization, and so can be seen as our own self-induced limits to the freedom to choose.

Jean-Paul Sartre (1905–80)

Jean-Paul Sartre, together with his contemporary Merleau-Ponty, reflected the modern French approach to existentialism. Sartre's views on free will and freedom of choice, as well as his attitude to relationships and relatedness, all form potentially key elements in a mediator's understanding of parties in conflict.

In his influential work *Existentialism Is a Humanism*, given first as a lecture in 1945, Sartre proposed the important thesis that *existence precedes essence*. This is how he himself described it in a lecture:

> What do we mean by saying that existence precedes essence? We mean that man first of all exists, encounters himself, surges up in the world – and defines himself afterwards. If man as the existentialist sees him is not definable, it is because to begin with he is nothing. He will not be anything until later, and then he will be what he makes of himself.
>
> From *Existentialism from Dostoevsky to Sartre*,
> ed. Walter Kaufman, Meridian Publishing Company, 1989,
> trans. P. Mairet

The manner in which man defines himself is through making choices and through the exercise of the free will to choose. For Sartre there is no such thing as 'human nature'; rather, man makes of himself what he chooses and what he wills. This is the true freedom. There is freedom to choose, but also the freedom *not* to choose or to refuse to make a choice: this is itself a significant choice. But the choices are not confined to acts – what to do now, what to do first, or what or how to do next. They encompass also the freedom to interpret: to make interpretations of our situation, of facts both past and present; of the statements of others and of their motivations: in effect, it is the freedom to interpret the entire outside world and the manner in which we propose to interact with it.

This freedom to choose, however, has to be measured against man's ultimate choice: the choice of death (through suicide). It is only when man is confronted with this realization – the freedom to choose life or death – that his freedom of choice is put in its proper perspective. The freedom to choose life, of course, includes in particular the freedom to choose how we live our lives. Such a freedom therefore also brings with it a heavy responsibility. One cannot be exercised without the other. This connection between freedom and responsibility is a constant factor in existentialist thought, and is a very relevant and important feature for any mediator to consider when facilitating parties in dispute. As Victor Frankl so aptly put it: 'I recommend that the Statue of Liberty on the East Coast be supplemented by a Statue of Responsibility on the West Coast' (2004: 134).

The freedom is so fundamental as to be inescapable: man cannot shirk his responsibility constantly to choose, and in this way is 'condemned' to this freedom. Sartre describes it in this way:

> That is what I mean when I say that man is condemned to be free. Condemned, because he did not create himself, yet is nevertheless at liberty, and from the moment that he is thrown into this world he is responsible for everything he does.
>
> (Sartre, quoted in Kaufman, ed.., 1989)

Sartre's examination of the responsibility of choice leads us fittingly into a glimpse of his outlook on relationships and relatedness. In *Being and Nothingness* he refers to 'the Other' as the person with the capacity to make judgments about ourselves, and through whose observation or 'look' (*le regard*) and by whose judgments our own being is defined.

> The Other's look fashions my body in its nakedness, causes it to be born, sculptures it, produces it as it is, sees it as I shall never see it. The Other holds a secret – the secret of what I am.
>
> (1956: 475)

Chapter 4 of this book examines more closely the concept of self-esteem, and demonstrates the vital role played by the notion that others are constantly observing us, and by our concern that in so 'looking ' at us, they are making judgments about us. It is therefore not difficult to understand the reason for Sartre's view that the Other, and our relationship with and relatedness to one another, is a principal cause of conflict. '*L'enfer, c'est les autres*', or 'Hell is other people', is a common descriptive interpretation of Sartre's play *Huis Clos* (literally 'Closed Door' or 'No Exit'), in which three deceased people are locked in a room for eternity. Each of the three characters in the play constitutes a threat to the actualization of the other's aspirations; each character's view of themselves is dependent upon the judgment and perception of the other – and this is their punishment. Sartre's view of relatedness as being closely aligned with conflict is perhaps a sad legacy, and is in contrast to Heidegger's proposition that our relationship with others is a source of potential opportunities and 'endless possibilities'. 'For Heidegger, such a form of relating helps the other to open up their possibilities for being, and to exist in a more authentic manner' (Cooper, 2003: 20).

Existentialism and *Ubuntu*

While dealing with the existentialist view of relationships and relatedness, it may be rewarding to digress momentarily, and to compare existentialism with the principles of *Ubuntu*, a South African philosophy dating back to the mid-nineteenth century. Regent's University London has formed a collaboration with the Desmond Tutu Foundation, and the principles of *Ubuntu* have more recently been expounded and promoted by Archbishop Desmond Tutu. *Ubuntu* is an African Bantu term roughly translated as 'humanity', and in the philosophical sense means humanity towards others. This traditional African philosophy approximates extraordinarily closely to existentialism and the ideas of Heidegger. It emphasizes man's common humanity; the connectedness and interdependence of man as a human being. A frequently quoted definition of *Ubuntu*, sometimes ascribed to Nelson Mandela, is: 'I am what I am because of who we all are.' In similar vein, in a speech in 2008, Archbishop Tutu described *Ubuntu* as:

> the essence of being human. *Ubuntu* speaks particularly about the fact that you can't exist as a human being in isolation. It speaks about our interconnectedness. You can't be human all by yourself.

Existence, as has been stated above, is fundamentally relational, and existentialism, like *Ubuntu*, similarly demonstrates how our 'relatedness' creates the coping mechanisms and strategies we adopt in order to exist in the world; it shows how we interact with one another in human relationships. The principles of both *Ubuntu* and existentialism encourage us to look beyond ourselves and to become more fully human.

Conclusion

The diagram below, taken and adapted from Strasser and Randolph (2004: 172), identifies some of the attributes that are shared by all mankind, irrespective of their race, colour, nationality, ethnic or geographical background. It may be worth mentioning, albeit as a departure from purist existential thinking, that the commonalities of our existence are also supported on a wholly different and scientific basis. A survey led by Professor Marcus Feldman of Stanford University (the results of which were published in the journal *Science* on 22 December 2002) showed that human beings share 99.9 per cent of their DNA. When our shared existential attributes are interwoven with our common DNA, it is perhaps not surprising that similar or matching human traits may be recognized in all persons – and parties in conflict are no exception.

Some of the shared existential givens have been touched upon in previous pages in relation to the manner in which they are presented by the existentialist philosophers in their respective works. These and some of the remaining shared characteristics depicted in the

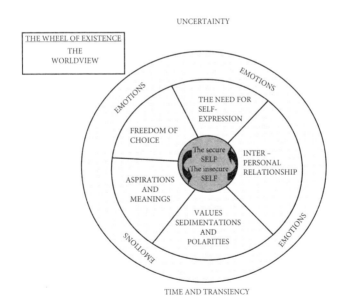

The diagram represents a non-chronological and non-linear interconnection of some existential givens

diagram will be examined further in subsequent chapters. Although considered separately in distinct chapters, the common human features are each interwoven with one another, and each implicate the other. An element of repetition is inevitable.

2

The Role of the Mediator – A Psychological Perspective

Throughout this book the term 'mediator' is used to encompass all those involved in conflict, whether in the form of conflict avoidance, conflict management or conflict resolution. The term will therefore cover not only the accredited and professional mediator, but will also incorporate lawyers, diplomats, politicians, national leaders, HR executives, police officers, hostage negotiators and many others who are called upon to assist or intervene in, negotiate or manage conflict. This will embrace commercial, international, or workplace disputes, as well as simply social and domestic quarrels.

The Role of the Mediator

The starting point in properly appreciating the role of the mediator is to question the mediator's true function: what is the most fundamental aspect of the mediator's work when managing or resolving conflict? Stripped down to a bare essential, the single most vital objective of a mediator is to secure an attitude shift on the part of one or more of the parties in the conflict. Without such a change in attitude, the parties are likely to remain in the same entrenched positions as when they entered the conflict, creating little prospect of settling their dispute. As is often stated by mediators: 'We cannot change the dispute but we can change our attitude towards it.' Put another way: 'If we change the way we look at things, the things we look at change' – 'an ancient Tao observation', according to Wayne W. Dyer, an American psychologist, in *A New Way of Thinking, a New Way of Being: Experiencing the Tao Te Ching* (2009); but it is also a quote sometimes attributed to Max Planck, the twentieth-century German physicist.

The shift of attitude will be fundamentally one of perception. The requisite perceptions that need to change may relate to crucially vital elements at the very heart of the dispute, or they may be entirely peripheral; they may be directed at another person in the conflict, or at that person's behaviour, or at the motivations for their behaviour. The perceptions may be intra personal, involving a change in the party's own self-awareness and self-concept. Alternatively, the requisite change in perception might be far removed from personalities and may relate instead to a party's expectations as to the outcome of the dispute – the amount of money to be recovered, or the level of capitulation on the part of the other disputant. Any such modifications of outlook, however small, may nevertheless be significant in precipitating a narrowing of the gap between the contesting parties. The mediator thus seeks gently to nudge the parties to move to a different perception – of themselves, of each other and of the dispute.

Securing such a shift in perception or attitude is not easy. Parties will have held their views about the matters in dispute, as well as about the persons involved, for weeks, months, or perhaps even years and decades. Their positions will have hardened over that period, as they maintain and protect their standpoints; their mindsets will have become increasingly entrenched as they defend their views. These views may have become further solidified as a result of comments and advice received from friends, family, lawyers and experts. This entourage of people will in turn have based their observations and counsel upon a diet of one-sided and subjective views emanating from one or other of the parties. Equally, the parties in dispute may have developed a complete 'block' and become wholly impervious to the contrary observations and exhortations of those around them. It is perhaps unsurprising that parties approach disputes in such states of intransigence. Yet despite this environment of rigid and 'sedimented' positions, the mediator will nevertheless be expected to secure a paradigm shift in hardened attitudes – and, further, will need to do so within the relatively short space of time allotted to the mediation.

Not Through Logic

The first realization for the psychologically informed mediator is that a perception shift will not be achieved through the application of logic or reason. Rational argument and logical persuasion have little or no effect in such conflict situations – and, indeed, may be counter-productive. It is futile for the mediator to wag a finger at a party in dispute and exhort them to change their attitude. When parties are in conflict, they are rarely in a frame of mind to listen to reason: they appear neither to think nor to behave *rationally* or *logically*. (An explanation for this phenomenon is set out in the following chapter on Emotions). The parties' perceptions will be poles apart, each fervently believing that their own perception is and can be the only real truth. Those in dispute frequently offer up a prayer: a hope that 'common sense will prevail'. Such prayers are rarely answered: there may well be considerable sense on display, but rarely will it be common. Each party will have a wholly different perception of 'the truth', and will at the same time zealously hold theirs to be the only possible genuine, objective, universal, accurate and undeniable truth. The philosophical approach to the absence of 'objective truth' is one adopted by many existentialists, in particular by Kierkegaard, and has already been examined in some detail in the previous chapter.

The variety of perceptions that can exist in any one given situation was aptly epitomized by the American comic George Carlin when he said: 'Have you ever noticed when you are driving on the freeway, that anyone who is driving slower than you is an idiot, and anyone driving faster than you is a maniac?' In this scenario, the three drivers each perceive the other to be either an idiot or a maniac, while at the same time perceiving themselves to be entirely normal. Consequently, in a situation where three persons occupy three metaphorical 'lanes of a motorway', there will be nine different perceptions of the very same state of being: the idiot in one person's view is the maniac in another's, while normal in his own perception – and vice versa. These patterns of outlook and behaviour will readily be recognized by those involved in 'shuttle' models of mediation: each party expresses a view of the other as the idiot or alternatively as the maniac, while urging all – and in particular the mediator – to believe that they themselves are the only normal, reasonable and rational people in the dispute.

Lawyers may similarly encounter the futility of rational and logical argument when dealing both with their opponents as well as with their own clients. Lawyers frequently find themselves in the position of having to advise their clients to abandon their claims or to withdraw their defences to claims. The client's case may be factually weak, or legally unsustainable, or evidentially problematic. Yet persuading clients to follow such advice is invariably challenging. They are unable to take a dispassionate or businesslike view; they are more intent upon pursuing an emotional route towards possible vindication. They adopt these stances irrespective of the prospects of success, regardless of the potential costs that will be incurred, and heedless of the time that will inevitably be lost: 'I don't care how much it costs; I don't mind how long it takes; I just want to sue the so-and-so' is a common refrain from many clients. Similarly with the lawyer's opponents: take, for example, the position of a lawyer who carefully sets out his client's case in what he regards as a beautifully crafted, cogently argued, logically persuasive letter, containing a comprehensive and coherent analysis of his client's position. Both the lawyer and the client will be convinced that the letter is so reasonable, and its logic so plausibly unassailable, that it cannot fail to persuade the other side of the errors of their case. How naïve: rarely does it succeed in this way. The other party is unlikely suddenly to capitulate, in a spontaneous and miraculous realization of their failure to see the situation in the correct light: 'My goodness, we never looked at it like that – they must be right.' Rather, the contrary is true: the letter is likely to precipitate a reply, similarly cogently and rationally argued, twice as long, seeking to dismiss each and every point made in the first letter, but with even more extreme, divergent and defensive arguments being put forward. No doubt such a response is also written in a similar belief that the arguments submitted are quite impossible to refute. Indeed, it is a sad paradox for lawyers to realize that the more logical and the more persuasive their argument, the more contrary and extreme will be the response. This may explain the exasperation frequently expressed by legal advisers, that they are unable to make either their opponents, or even their own clients, 'see sense'.

Perceiving Commonalities

One of the functions of a mediator is to dispel the *mis*perceptions and *false* assumptions held by parties in the conflict (see Chapter 7). The polarization and diversity of perceptions by those in dispute is inescapable. The 'Us and Them', the 'I and You', and 'the Other' are habitual patterns of thought and expression in conflict, and are common themes in existentialist philosophy. The existence of and our relationship with 'the Other' is an important and recurring topic among existentialists; the concept of our relatedness has been considered in the previous chapter and is examined further below (see Chapter 6). Polarity of thought and perception is more prevalent than unity and commonality. But even where unity and commonality exist they are relatively short-lived: there will inevitably come a time when any such unity is subjected to question and challenge. This is a common factor throughout all groupings, whether corporate organizations, democratic states, political parties, sports teams, or domestic households: unity of thought and deed may prevail for a period, but there will inevitably come a time when a faction challenges or separates from the majority, and conflict is the result. Hegel, the eighteenth-century German philosopher, is remembered for identifying this perpetual cycle of unity followed by challenge as a dialectic triad. He referred to the concepts of *thesis, antithesis and synthesis* – where *thesis* represents the unity or status quo; *antithesis* is the challenge to that status quo; and *synthesis* the new product resulting from the conflict between the two.

Wherever such a challenge to the status quo arises, there will be distinctly polarized views on either side of the divide (for polarities, see Chapter 5). Each will regard them self as normal and the other as the 'idiot' or the 'maniac'. For example, in elections or referendums, those holding views and opinions on one side will regard theirs as sensible, coherent and realistic, whereas those expressed by the other will be characterized as absurd, illogical and unreasonable. Divorcing parents will view their own position as reasonable, and that of the other as extreme and untenable; corporate entities locked in contractual litigation will believe that their stance is entirely in keeping with the contract and utterly commercial, whereas that of the other is in flagrant breach of the agreement and wholly lacking in business intelligence.

In many of these instances, the parties may nevertheless share a common aim or purpose, but simply harbour a *difference of opinion* as to how that objective may best be achieved. The electorate on opposing sides of an election or referendum may have similar aims, namely to secure that which is best for the good of themselves, of the country and of the nation as a whole; they merely disagree upon which party is most likely to accomplish it. Divorcing parents will often have the best interests of their children at heart, but have deep and divided convictions as to which of them is better placed to achieve those interests. And, similarly, corporate entities each seek ultimately to make profit, and each believe they have discovered the optimum means of so doing, but may believe the other is actively impeding them in that endeavour.

In all these examples it might benefit the parties not to lose sight of the fact that, at least in some respects, they are all on 'the same side'; that they all have common aims; and that they are merely labouring under the burden of a *difference of opinion*. If the mediator is able to sow the seed of this notion while also assisting a party in dispelling the view that the other is seeking to achieve the common aim *at their expense*, both sides of the conflict can begin to develop a more constructive and collaborative attitude. A constructive perception of the commonalities of their situation can bring them to a fruitful realization that it is not so much a dispute, but more a differing approach towards the same goal. The conflict may then be seen as less of an obstacle in the relationship and more of a transforming energy for their mutual good (see further Chapter 5, for common values).

Communication Skills to Achieve Perception Shift

If an alteration of perception is such a vital element of any dispute resolution process, and if it cannot be achieved through reason and logic, we need to consider how this seemingly impossible challenge can be addressed by a mediator. In the following chapters, an attempt is made at providing an explanation for the reason parties in conflict are so resistant to logic and rational argument. We will see that invariably it is a highly emotional state of mind that clouds the judgment and prevents parties from listening to reason; and that this in turn is related to a person's values and value systems, and to their self-esteem and self-concept. For the mediator effectively to penetrate this ostensibly solid wall of resistance, it is necessary for the mediator first to disarm the anger, absorb the emotions so as to enable the passions to subside and so move the parties to a platform where they are more amenable to reason, and are ready to listen. For this, a number of skills and techniques are required. The skills are largely communication skills: the ability to allow the parties to be and to feel truly heard, through 'actively listening', and the capacity to build a trusting relationship and create a strong rapport with those in dispute. There can be no more powerful a tool for the creation of a trusting relationship and the building of rapport than for the mediator to prove that he or she is truly and faithfully listening. This vital skill is a *sine qua non* of the mediator's tool kit, which, when sensitively deployed, can enable the mediator more effectively to challenge and reality-test, and thereby achieve that vital perception shift.

'Safe' Environment and Trust and Rapport

The invaluable benefit of building trust and creating rapport is that through this, the mediator can provide a safe environment in which the parties to the dispute can more openly and candidly express their views. The 'safe' environment is not necessarily one of physical safety, but, rather, the creation of a setting in which there is an absence of judgment: where the parties feel free of criticism, do not fear denigration, condemnation or reproach. A trusting relationship makes it easier for the mediator to defuse the hostility and to absorb the antagonistic emotions permeating the dispute. The empathic affinity created by rapport will further enable the mediator effectively to challenge and to reality-test. Any hint of disapproval by the mediator before a trusting relationship has developed may trigger an immediate closing down and defensiveness on the part of the person on the receiving end; the mediator will simply become just another person in a long line of those who 'do not understand'. The resulting atmosphere will not be conducive to the resolution of the dispute. Without a bond of connection, the mediator will find it difficult, if not impossible, to precipitate the requisite attitude shift in the mind of the disputant. It is a well-recognized fact that we will much more readily accept advice from a friend than from a stranger – particularly if that advice is unpalatable. Hence the effective mediator needs to be a friend or 'comrade' – from the Spanish word *camarada*, meaning room-mate – someone who metaphorically shares the same room as the party in conflict.

The building of these closer relationships invariably takes time. In contexts outside the arena of mediation, such relationships and rapport will usually develop over several meetings, often in a social setting, with an amenable and pleasant ambience and in relaxed and agreeable surroundings. In the context of disputes, however, the mediator is likely to encounter the parties in a hostile environment, in a stressful and emotionally charged atmosphere, in surroundings which, even if entirely neutral, may nevertheless still seem alien and unfriendly. The parties are tense, anxious and apprehensive – and often mistrustful of all around them. Their emotions may be raw, and their state of mind entirely averse to any form of rapprochement with their perceived enemy. All these factors militate against the easy creation of trust. A yet further factor for the mediator to address is that there is not the luxury of time to overcome these dynamics: the mediator needs to develop trust and rapport almost instantaneously, from the very first moment of any encounter.

The Skills

The ability and capacity instantaneously to create trust and rapport is rarely intuitive; more frequently, it is the product of intense and meticulous training. The communication skills that need to be deployed are in fact counter-intuitive: they are, regrettably, rarely seen in our everyday interactions. We do not listen properly: we listen from a selfish perspective, based upon what we think we need to know, rather than listening in order to hear what others have to say. We make little attempt to let the other person know that we are listening. Indeed, the English idiom 'I hear what you say' means exactly the opposite – 'I do not hear what you say'. And we have a persistent urge to interrupt, thereby further reinforcing the message, 'I am not interested in what you have to say; in fact I am not interested in listening to you at all'.

This may not be the place to consider in any detail the particular skills taught to prospective mediators on mediation accreditation courses, such as the Mediation Skills course at Regent's University London. However, it may be informative to set out a selection of the criteria listed in RUL's Assessment Guidance Notes as demonstrating some of the essential communication skills that are looked for when assessing students for accreditation as mediators:

- showing impartiality
- displaying empathy
- good 'positive' listening
- good non-verbal communication (for example, silence, eye contact)
- good verbal communication (for example, non-judgmental language)
- using open questions
- paraphrasing, summarizing, reflecting
- good use of 'laddering/unpacking/deconstructing'
- alert to recurring themes, hidden agendas, signals and clues
- probing, challenging and reality-testing appropriately
- aware of 'value systems'
- exploring the underlying basis of emotions
- exploring tensions and anger
- encouraging and not demoralizing
- sensitive use of interventions.

From a psychological perspective, it is important to note that these criteria are virtually all directed towards one aspect: namely, allowing the other party to feel properly *heard*. Thus communication skills, while axiomatic in building trust and rapport, are also inextricably bound together with the ability to allow parties to feel comprehensively 'listened to'. Many disputes are a result of people feeling that no one is listening; that they have no proper voice, and they have simply not been heard. Consequently, the only option that invariably appears available to them is to enter into 'dispute mode'. Whether it is a consumer making a complaint, neighbours arguing over a party wall, a corporate entity negotiating in respect of a broken contract, or a political entity manoeuvring for recognition – if any of them believe they are deprived of a voice, or, if given a voice, one to which they feel that no one is listening, they will find themselves in a conflict situation and may resort to the traditional means of resolution: litigation or war.

The magical power of mediation lies in the ability of the mediator to allow the parties to feel truly heard. In many instances, the party at the mediation table will experience for the very first time in his or her life the true nature and value of *really being listened to*. A party who feels heard can rarely sustain that anger for any length of time: the concentrated listening skills of the mediator will defuse the anger. The party in dispute who feels he or she has been undervalued, taken for granted, or ignored will blissfully appreciate the fact that, at last, the mediator is respecting them and taking them seriously. There can be no greater catalyst to the creation of trust and rapport than to allow a person to feel thoroughly and empathically heard.

The most powerful skills that can be deployed by a listener to ensure that the speaker feels truly heard are those of 'reflecting back', paraphrasing and summarizing. Mediators sometimes underestimate the psychologically persuasive quality that these listening 'techniques' have for creating a connection with the speaker. For someone to have the exact words they have used reflected back to them verbatim is a formidable demonstration of listening. Yet, further, to have their own words given back to them *paraphrased* – that is, in the personal words of the mediator – generates an even greater compelling boost to their self-esteem. For it demonstrates that the mediator has not only listened and understood, but has absorbed what has been said, has processed the words and meanings given, and has returned those words to the speaker in the mediator's own thoughtful interpretation. There may be little more flattering or gratifying to a speaker than to have such close attention paid to what has been said.

These skills of listening may be in sharp contrast to the manner in which we listen in our everyday lives. We approach the task of information gathering in a very different way, whether or not we are lawyers or other professionals. We tend to elicit information that we regard as necessary for our specific purposes. Lawyers, for example, will solicit facts in order to understand the dispute and diligently to prepare and develop their client's case. They 'listen' by asking a series of largely factual questions in order to achieve a narrow and specific objective. Yet this may not be the most effective way for any of us to elicit the required data. If mediators were simply to ask a series of questions, it would approximate to an interrogation and would do little to build rapport. Indeed, such questioning can be counter-productive, in that the party may feel that they are being analytically examined rather than being fully and properly listened to. It might be a more fruitful exercise to ask fewer questions and instead to reflect back, paraphrase and summarize what the party has said.

These skills, as indicated by the American psychologist Carl Rogers, in his rhetorical approach to 'person-centred' therapy, represent important tools for active and effective listening. Although they may be termed 'techniques', if and when used naturally and non-mechanistically they can be the most powerful skills for creating trust and rapport. With the contents of this toolbox, the mediator may be better equipped to move parties in the direction of settlement and resolution.

3

Emotions

All conflict involves people, and so all conflict is inevitably 'personal'. Without people, there would be no conflict, and people are never without emotions. So emotions are ever-present. Philosophers have long pondered the phenomena of emotions, seeking to define them and debating as to whether they are to be associated with the body and bodily 'instincts', or with the rational processes of the mind. Existentialists tend to refer to emotions as *feelings* and *moods*, and contend that it is through these that we are rendered fully aware of our existence. In *Existentialism*, John Macquarrie describes Plato's view of emotions as 'feelings' in this simple way:

> Feeling seems to lie somewhere between the mere life-processes of the body, of some of which we are barely conscious or even unconscious, and the conscious exercise of rational thought.
>
> (1972: 158)

To others, emotions are simply a well-recognized biological phenomenon.

> Hard-wired basic affects such as the fearful fight or flight reaction, or its opposite, pleasurable approach, are the bedrock

on which elaborated emotions build. Our primordial emotions are universal, biologically based response systems that have enabled humans to meet the problems of physical survival, reproduction, and group governance.

Deutsch, Coleman and Marcus (2006: 271)

Through the ages, philosophers and psychologists have sought to identify and categorize emotions, and the numbers recognized have ranged from as few as four basic emotions to as many as 130 or more. Irrespective of how emotions are classified, there is little doubt that they form an integral part of our behavioural strategies in everyday existence. The ever-present nature of emotions as a shared and common 'given' among all human beings is helpful to the mediator. Consequently they are of fundamental importance when dealing with conflict, and it is suggested that a mediator cannot perform effectively without a thorough appreciation of the nature and effect of emotions. We need to understand how they inform our behaviour; how best to manage them when they present themselves in parties in mediation; and how to channel them for the constructive benefit of conflict resolution.

Reflective or Unreflective

Some debate has centred on the question as to whether emotions can further be characterized as 'reflective' and 'unreflective', terms taken from Jean Paul Sartre. Unreflective emotions can be described as instantaneous, and are those over which we have little or no control: they can neither be conjured up at will nor dispelled deliberately or consciously. Fear, anger, disgust and passion are examples of unreflective emotion; on the other hand, guilt, shame and jealousy may be seen as reflective. Strasser argues (1999: 24) that such categorization is feasible, and seeks to differ from Sartre's view, as expressed in his *Sketch for a Theory of Emotions* (1962), that all emotions are unreflective. Indeed, Sartre postulates that the moment an emotion becomes 'reflective' it ceases to be an emotion. The distinction between reflective and unreflective emotions may, however, be important to the mediator. By their very nature, as described by Strasser, reflective emotions are likely to be amenable to reflective and conscious thought. A mediator may be in a position to assist a party to analyse a reflective emotion, and through such analysis to mould a perception shift. Unreflective emotions, on the other hand, may be impermeable and resistant to any useful analysis. Such emotions may need to be accepted by the mediator in a non-judgmental manner, so that they may be absorbed, defused and possibly deflected.

Any examination of people's emotions, however, is rendered more difficult by the fact that rarely is there only one emotion being experienced or manifested at any one time. Emotions tend to be 'layered', with several emotions featuring at the same time. These may be described as foreground and background emotions. For example, we may feel anger, which is in the foreground, while at the same time experiencing sadness, in the background. It is also likely that we will have emotions about emotions, or emotional responses to emotions. We can experience frustration and disappointment, while being angry at feeling disappointed and frustrated; yet, further, we may experience a sense of guilt at the fact that we are angered by the frustration or disappointment. This conglomeration of emotions is a fertile area for exploration by all those involved in conflict management. In many instances, parties will be confused about their emotions, struggling to understand their source or their target. Some may not even be aware of the various emotional drivers in themselves. A party in a boundary dispute may be asked: 'Your neighbour has moved the boundary fence two centimetres into your property – what element of that causes you such distress and anger?' The response may be confused, with the party unclear, for example, as to whether it is the loss of two centimetres of land or the audacity on the part of the neighbour in failing to consult with them. The party may even be wholly unaware of the true source of their anger; and they may be surprised at what they discover when invited to engage in some introspection. It is through an analysis of these feelings that a helpful level of a disputant's self-awareness can be achieved. This in turn may accelerate the requisite change of attitude in the parties that might bring them closer to an end of the conflict.

Emotions are Revelatory

An understanding of the object at which a person's emotions are directed can significantly assist the mediator in managing the conflict. It is therefore helpful to appreciate that *all* emotions, whether reflective or not, are 'intentional' – a phenomenological use of the word, indicating that emotions are always directed at something or some specific condition or state. We cannot be emotional in a vacuum; there will always be an object or target to our emotions: we will be angry *about* another's behaviour, or fearful *of* a state of affairs, or joyful *because of* something. So when a party to a dispute displays emotion, it will be worthy of exploration by the mediator as it is likely to be highly revelatory. In the above example of the neighbour dispute, the exploration of the object of the presented emotion may assist in revealing the true core of the dispute – to the party themselves as well as to the mediator.

Anger and Loss

Anger, for example, is an extremely common emotion in conflict situations, and is invariably precipitated by some form of loss. It may be actual, potential, past, present or future loss. It may be about tangible matters – loss of money, property, land or other objects. Alternatively, the loss can represent something more metaphysical, such as time, energy, or control. Very often, it involves the loss of an envisaged future: hopes, dreams and aspirations anticipated in the future that now seem lost. Hence, when parties are called upon to compromise, the prospect of the loss of such elements will invariably create anger. Our aversion to loss affects our freedom to choose: we are fearful of making a choice that might result in a loss; and hence our anxiety at having to make these choices in the face of such uncertainty is greatly heightened.

The revelatory nature of emotions is habitually overlooked or underestimated by mediators. They often seek to suppress or control the emotions of those in a dispute. Mediators will occasionally attempt to 'coach' parties into behaving in a restrained manner in any joint meetings that take place at a mediation or negotiation table (see further Chapter 8). Parties are urged to avoid being confrontational; to say little that may be in any way adversarial; not to utter things that may unduly inflame or provoke the other side. This, it is suggested, is not only often unnecessary, but it may also be counter-productive. The display of emotions is likely to reveal the roots of the dispute: what it is that triggered such anger; what it was that caused such hurt, grief, sorrow, disappointment, betrayal, alienation or loss of trust. These are the realities of the conflict: so why should the mediator shield parties from this reality? It is neither required nor is it helpful to protect parties from the emotions that form the very essence of and underpin the entirety of the conflict.

The Anglo-Saxon temperament is quite averse to demonstrations of emotion. We are uncomfortable in their presence; and, in extreme instances, we can often be quite alarmed by their appearance. We shall see in later chapters that this is largely due to our need to be and remain in control. The unpredictability of people's behaviour under high emotions evokes an anxiety in us because we are unsure as to how to deal with it. The principal concern of all those present – the mediator, the parties, their legal advisers and any others in attendance – is likely to be directed at the uncertainty and unpredictability of the outcome: 'This is getting out of control; where will it all lead?' In courts, judges and lawyers are equally apprehensive: the witness who breaks down with emotion in the witness box will be offered a glass of water, seemingly the panacea for all such situations. The mediator confronted by an exhibition of emotion will often suggest a short break; the lawyers and others present in the room may feel equally discomforted at the sight of a person in tears or in rage, and may also ask for a brief adjournment.

The mediator, however, can profit from taking the time to explore and investigate such displays of emotions when they are presented. Such exploration is not an invasive procedure: it may scratch a little beneath the surface, but it does not involve 'digging' for emotions. The mediator does no more than to further investigate the emotions that have already surfaced and have been revealed. This examination of the underlying feelings of a party in conflict is not a digression, but is, rather, a vital exercise for any existentially informed mediator. It is a central plank of most existentialist thinking that it is not the facts that are important but, rather, how we *experience* those facts from an emotional standpoint. We will see in Chapter 5 how our emotions are closely interrelated with our values, our value systems and self-concepts. Emotions are a most reliable and informative means of disclosing our values, the values being the principles we hold dear and by which we live. It is the way in which these values are affected, whether impeded or advanced, that will precipitate an emotion. For example, a person who has a value system based upon loyalty will experience a variety of emotions when confronted by disloyalty. These emotions are likely to be absent or non-effective in a person to whom loyalty is not a value and has no significance.

The mediator's examination as to the source or object of a party's emotional experience will disclose a wealth of information: the emotions are the 'royal road' to their worldview – where the worldview consists of their values, beliefs and assumptions about themselves, about others and about the world in general.

All Conflict is Emotional

People frequently deceive themselves into believing that their dispute is devoid of emotion. Parties and their lawyers will seek to proclaim that the dispute is 'not personal', but is purely commercial – 'it's just about the money'. They insist that they are approaching the conflict 'purely from an economic standpoint'. Yet there is no dispute, however 'dry' or purely commercially oriented, that is without a significant emotional content. Most disputes spring from some perceived injustice, and this will inevitably involve injury to feelings. This injury is aggravated by the fact that many conflicts often involve allegations of 'fault': a breach of contract or an act of negligence amounts to a serious accusation of fault, and can create deep and powerful emotions. Incursions into another's territory will generate even greater perceptions of injustice. Indeed, all transgressions of another's values – the beliefs and ideologies that they treasure – will result in powerful emotions. In the same way, the denial of these allegations or of fault will produce equal or even greater frustration, irritation and upset. Hence a potent motivator in conflict is frequently the need for the other party to 'say sorry': to accept fault, admit liability and take responsibility for their actions. (See Chapter 4, Self-esteem, and the problematic nature of the word 'sorry').

Most conflicts have one common thread: a request or demand followed by a refusal. Each demand will invariably involve a rational element, driven by commercial, economic, political, or religious need or want: 'We want this because we have suffered a specific economic or other loss'. The demand will also contain an emotional element, driven by feelings of anger, hurt, betrayal or a sense of perceived injustice: 'We want this because they should not be permitted to get away with such conduct.' Equally, the rejection of a request or the refusal to give in to the demand will similarly be driven by commercial features – 'Their claim is inflated' – alongside emotional components – 'They are trying to manipulate us'. If it were possible to take the emotional element out of the conflict, and approach every dispute from a purely rational, practical, pragmatic or commercial standpoint, very few disputes would continue to exist: they would be resolved mathematically, geometrically, geographically – or simply logically. The Greek philosopher Aristotle (384–322 bc) identified the divisive element of emotions: without emotions, logic produces only one end result; the logical thread, if followed through, arrives at only one conclusion. It is emotion that causes the divide: emotions create differing perspectives of the same 'truth'. In other words, it is the emotional content that escalates a mere difference of opinion into an intense dispute.

Conflicts are not Rational

It is constructive for the mediator to understand how these emotions affect or inform the behaviour of parties in a dispute. We have noted that the psychologically informed mediator will appreciate that parties in conflict do not behave rationally, logically or commercially. Frequently, as we have also noted, the parties may not even recognize their own underlying emotions: they may believe that their demand for 'damages in compensation' is utterly logical, reasonable, equitable, rational and commercial: nothing other than simply a desire for proper redress or recompense. They are unwilling to accept that in fact their demand for money is driven by emotions such as anger, or hurt, or a desire to punish and humiliate. Just as lawyers often fail to appreciate the futility of seeking to persuade others through logic or rational legalistic argument, so also do mediators frequently underestimate the influence of emotions upon behaviour. It is rarely effective to rely purely upon cogent and logically persuasive arguments in order to secure a perception shift in either of the parties. Kierkegaard's dismissal of the concept of 'objective truth' demonstrates how opposing sides in a conflict situation will honestly and genuinely believe their own perception to represent the only objective truth. 'The notion of an absolute or final truth that exists independently of a human perspective is not credible' (Iacovou and Weixel-Dixon, 2015: 64).

The parties to a dispute do not hold a monopoly on emotions. It is not only they who may be affected by emotions, but the emotions can often spill over into the psyche of their legal advisers. A survey of company executives and in-house lawyers, conducted in the UK in 2007 by solicitors Field Fisher Waterhouse, showed that 47 per cent of respondents admitted that a personal dislike of their opponent had led them into prolonged, and costly, litigation.

Aristotle was one of the first to identify the internal struggle between emotions and reason, believing that humans were the only beings capable of rational thought, whereas animals were driven by emotions. In this way, he is interpreted as having created the view that emotions are inferior to reason, whereas this may not be entirely correct. Aristotle, alongside other Athenian philosophers, 'used the concept that emotion is primitive, animalistic, unintelligent and dangerous – and hence needed to be controlled by reason – to justify the concept of slavery' (Solomon: 2008). This has, rightly or wrongly, left us with the 'master and slave' image of conflict: an eternal battle between reason and emotion, where reason is to be the 'master' conquering and subduing emotion which is seen as the 'slave'. In conflict, the reverse is invariably true: emotion is the master and reason the slave. Reason fails to control emotion; indeed, passion seems wholly to overwhelm logic. The greater the stakes and the more critical the outcome, the greater the emotion and the more scant the rational logic. When parties are in dispute, their ability to think rationally seems to diminish, if not completely disappear. The description of experiences such as 'the red mist descending' or 'I am so angry I cannot think straight' are not uncommon. It may also be characterized by a sudden loss of temper, or behaviour described as 'out of character' or even more extreme: 'losing it'. We often give advice to others to 'sleep on it' in order to feel differently the following day – and we do indeed have a differing perception in the cold light of a new day.

There is an anatomical and neurological explanation to this. It is not an explanation derived from existential philosophy, but comes with the benefit of advances in cognitive neuroscience, together with the research of Joseph LeDoux, an American neuroscientist. This research, coupled with our increased ability to monitor neural circuits in functional terms, has helped to reveal some of the architecture of the brain. These two together have allowed the following rationalization to be proposed. It is suggested that the answer lies in the existence of the amygdala, two small almond-shaped structures on either side of the brain, which govern our instinctive 'fight or flight' responses. The amygdala were formed in the earlier stages of the development of our brain and were a vital part of our evolution. By controlling our instinctive responses, they served to prevent a more time-consuming cerebral and analytical process that could prove fatal in the face of an imminent attack. We could not afford the time to analyse our options when under imminent attack: 'If I analyse my options, I believe I have four choices: I can jump to my right or I can jump to my left; I can retreat, or I can advance and fight.' Had we been obliged to undergo such analytical processes in the face of each and every danger, we as a species would doubtless not have survived. The amygdala (often referred to in the singular) intervene in such circumstances by 'taking control' of the reasoning brain, in order to produce a faster physical response. This phenomenon is sometimes referred to as an 'amygdala hijack', a term adapted from Daniel Coleman in *Emotional Intelligence* (1995), where he referred to emotional, limbic and neural hijackings. The amygdala receive sensory data through the eyes, the ears and the nose; and upon becoming aware of a threat of danger or attack divert the signals from the thalamus away from the neurological pathways to the cortex – the 'thinking' part of the brain – thereby avoiding the slow analytical procedures involved in making the right choice. Simultaneously, the amygdala precipitate chemical reactions in the body, by stimulating the production, secretion and circulation through the body of adrenalin, epinephrine and norepinephrine. Our heart rate and blood pressure are adjusted, and oxygen is pumped through the blood to support and aid the muscles. This neurological function was clearly vital for the survival of the species, in particular by serving to prevent 'paralysis through analysis'.

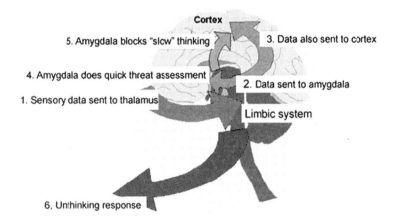

At first glance, the concept of an amygdala hijack may appear to be in direct conflict with the existential proposition that we all have freedom of choice. Yet it is important to note that when acting under the influence of the amygdala we are not conducting ourselves as automatons. The governing factor in our choice of fight or flight will always be our values and our value systems: there are those who instinctively act heroically in a threatening situation, whereas others will consider that 'the better part of valour is discretion' (Shakespeare: *Henry IV, Part 1*, Act V, Scene iv). Similarly the phenomenon whereby we 'see things differently the following day' can be explained from an existentialist as well

---

* Image taken from http://daniellebdefreitas.blogspot.co.uk/2014/04/theamygdala-hijack-and-me.html.

as a neurological perspective. The neurological rationalization is that the influence of the amygdala diminishes as the threat or danger recedes. The existentialist will argue that emotions are never static and are constantly changing. Consequently, our feelings will inevitably change after the elapse of any given period. Perhaps it is only necessary for a mediator to accept that these phenomena occur, without being persuaded as to their causation.

This 'hijacking' of the rational mind frequently occurs in the heightened emotional state of a bitter dispute, and creates an emotional and psychological barrier to settlement. Of course, nowadays, human beings are rarely faced with the type of physical attack that threatened the personal safety of our ancestors, such as from a wild animal. The attack is of a different kind, but one nevertheless perceived as equally dangerous and threatening. Any allegation of wrongdoing, whether of negligence or of a breach of contract, or any other imputation of fault, will involve some form of condemnation and disparagement, and will be sensed as being just as intimidating. Any form of criticism is capable of triggering an amygdala hijack; it is an attack upon integrity and upon self-esteem, and can produce similar defensive instincts (see Chapter 4, Self-esteem). Thus we see behaviour, for example, described as 'road rage', whereby normal, rational, sensible and otherwise restrained people suddenly appear to act 'out of character' and indulge in violent altercations. They will have perceived an attack that not only creates danger – 'The idiot could have killed me!' – but at the same time they see it as an affront to their perception of themselves as 'good drivers'. So instead of taking a balanced view – 'Poor chap, he failed to see me' – they become 'hijacked' into an instinctive 'fight or flight' mode of behaviour.

Finally, it must be noted that mediators will themselves be subject to the very same range of emotions as all those in dispute. Frustration and impatience are likely to be prominent at some stage in the process; anger may also bubble to the surface. Mediators are just as vulnerable to an amygdala hijack as any other. In such circumstances, it may assist them to remember the words of Aristotle, in *Nicomachean Ethics*:

> Anyone can become angry. That is easy. But to be angry with the right person, to the right degree, at the right time, for the right purpose, and in the right way, that is not easy.
>
> (Book II, 1109 a27)

4

Self-esteem

Self-esteem is one of the – if not *the* – most powerful motivating factors in all conflict in human existence. It governs much of our daily thinking and shapes many of our activities; it lies at the very heart of most disputes and is central to our behavioural strategies. It is one of the existential givens that all humans share: the fact that they possess a self-concept and self-esteem.

'The self' and our self-concept is a topic that has engaged many existentialist philosophers. We have seen how Kierkegaard sought to provide answers to the questions of who and what we are from a purely subjective standpoint. Heidegger approached the issue of 'the self' as one of relatedness, of 'being-in-the-world', and 'being-in-the-world-with-others'. However, it was Sartre, a pupil of Heidegger, who identified the importance of how others see us as shaping our own self-concept. In *Being and Nothingness*, Sartre proposes the notion that we can only become aware of who we are through the judgment ('*le regard*') of others.

The Need for Approval

The judgment of others is an intrinsic part of our relatedness and of being-in-the-world-with-others. We all have a strong need to be judged well – to think well of ourselves, to approve of the type of person we are and for ourselves to favour the actions we take. Consequently, it is important that others also think approvingly of us and of the activities we undertake. In this way, self-esteem governs the vast majority of the daily choices and the decisions we make. It ranges across the entire spectrum of options, from the most minor issues of daily existence to the very major life-changing questions. At the lower end of the spectrum, the entire cosmetic and fashion industries are built upon our need for approval to maintain our self-esteem: for example, it affects the selection of the clothes we wear each day, the perfume or aftershave we choose. This demonstrates the importance that we attach to how we are experienced by others. We choose the manner in which we project ourselves, and our entire behaviour and conduct towards others will be governed by the way we would like to be perceived by them. Self-esteem may therefore often govern decisions concerning the type of property and the location in which we choose to live, the car we drive and the friends we make. At the other end of the spectrum, it may be directed at the more fundamental values we create, for example, in selecting the moral and ethical way in which we wish to lead our lives, our career paths and the direction generally of our desired life's trajectory.

Self-esteem, however, is not static: it is constantly on the move. Although the need for approval and the fear of disapproval is constantly with us, our self-esteem can be raised, and it can very easily and quickly be lowered. Because of the fundamental part it plays in our everyday existence, an inordinate amount of time, effort and energy is expended by all of us in maintaining and protecting our self-esteem at a high level, while at the same time defending our self-worth from spiraling downwards. We are forever seeking the approval of others, and caring about the potential for their disapproval. It may therefore be plain to see why self-esteem plays such a vital role in all stages of a dispute: it plays a prominent part in the initial creation of the conflict; it shapes the conduct of those who find themselves in the middle of the dispute; and it is ultimately a critical influence in the way in which the dispute is resolved. It further explains the difficulties of securing an apology from another party. 'Sorry' is the word many aggrieved parties crave most strongly. It is at the same time an inexpensive, swift and easy means of addressing and resolving a perceived injustice. Yet it is almost impossible to extract the word from a litigant or disputing party. Our self-esteem does not allow us to admit fault for fear of the disapproval that such an admission creates in its wake. The instances of large corporations losing millions as a result of a simple failure or refusal to apologise are legion. It is their corporate self-esteem that creates the impediment to an apology.

Most of us will have some person or persons in the background whose approval is significant to us and whose disapproval we would wish to avoid. This is particularly so when we are in conflict. The entourage of people outside ourselves whose approval we seek may consist of an employer or line manager, a board of directors, trustees, a spouse or a partner, a parent or child or other relative, or simply a friend. There will always be someone within our contemplation upon whose judgment our self-esteem may hang. This is likely to be a factor in the initial creation of the conflict. A perceived injustice will have dented our self-esteem; some deed or word will have been taken as an offence or an insult; a breach of contract or an act of negligence will have been seen as an affront. All these affect our self-esteem: 'Who do they take me for? Who do they think I am?' Vindication and the ability to prove we are right can be a most attractive means of boosting our self-esteem: 'What better way to protect and restore my self-worth than to prove to everyone I am right?' The headlong drive into conflict is thus propelled and fuelled by our self-concept.

The person whose approval will be of prime and greatest importance to us, however, is our self. We have a perception of ourselves as we are and as we would like to be seen. This perception will be moulded by our values and value systems and will, in general, aim to be in line with the principles by which we have chosen to live. Consequently, we like to conduct ourselves in accordance with our self-concept: we are content with and approve of ourselves if our words, thoughts and deeds fall within the parameters of those values and principles. When, however, we find ourselves making choices that stray outside those boundaries, it inevitably affects our self-esteem. We would like to think of ourselves as highly principled, and would prefer to believe that our conduct is consistent, and undertaken only on an ethical and honourable basis. Hence parties will repeatedly confront the mediator with an insistence that their stance is the righteous one. This stance may often be one that is untenable from any proper commercial standpoint, but their self-esteem will not allow them to contravene the values they have created for themselves. For example, the leader of a corporate entity may acknowledge that to enter into, pursue or prolong a conflict or litigation is utterly uncommercial or entirely counter to the economic interests of the business; yet despite this, the conflict or litigation will be vigorously pursued, with the disputant shielding behind an insistence that their position is 'a matter of principle'.

It should not be overlooked that parties in dispute will also have an equally strong desire to secure the approval of the mediator at the mediation. However much mediators emphasize that they are entirely neutral, that they are neither judges nor arbitrators, and that they will not make judgments, the parties will nevertheless endeavour constantly to secure the mediator's approval. Their self-esteem will be heightened if they feel that the mediator is 'on their side': 'We are the reasonable, sensible, honourable, honest, truthful, and upright party here; it is the other side who are the very opposite of all these, and totally lacking in integrity.'

Fear of Disapproval

The corollary of our craving for the approval of others is an aversion to their disapproval. We do not wish to think badly of ourselves, and consequently we are concerned that others should not think the same. The 'look' of others (Sartre's '*le regard*') creates an inhibition to our self-concept that can cause considerable unease. Take, for example, public speaking: it has been suggested in various American surveys that speaking in public is one of our greatest fears – greater than that of flying or even of death. Why should that be? Why should the prospect of speaking to an audience, consisting of people whom we have never met, and whom we may never see again, be such a daunting prospect? The answer can be found in Sartre's '*le regard*': each member of that audience has the capacity to have 'the look' and therefore to make a judgment. Each person in the audience constitutes a single opportunity for disapproval: the opportunity to disagree with what we are saying; to spot our mistakes; to notice our memory failures; to ridicule us; and generally to think adversely of us. When such possible judgments are multiplied many times by the number of people in the audience, this can understandably lead to an overwhelming fear. The audience thus has the power to inflict the greatest level of disapproval, leading to our ultimate dread: humiliation.

In the context of a commercial dispute, the humiliation and disapproval come in the form of an accusation of negligence or breach of contract, or, still worse, of criminal or dishonest behaviour. There can be little more damaging to the self-esteem of those who believe they have conducted themselves impeccably, than to be faced with accusations of failure or misconduct. An allegation of negligence – a failure to act in a way in which all other reasonable persons would act – is hurtful and injurious; similarly, an assertion of a breach of contract – a deliberate disregard or flouting of a previous agreement – can be distressing. These contentions are made yet more damaging when accompanied by inferences of a more personal nature, such as dishonest, deceptive or fraudulent behaviour; or, worse still, where the contention imputes an element of personal betrayal. Yet allegations of such a nature populate the language of litigation. Letters sent by one party's lawyers to the other will be littered with wounding accusations of precisely such conduct. When read by the other party and their legal advisers, these accusations will inevitably be experienced as intense attacks upon self-esteem. Their coping mechanisms will come into play (see further below), and defensive modes of behaviour will be the result. Counter-attacks follow, and so the disputes escalate alarmingly. In conflict situations, the ultimate fear is that of humiliation. Our aversion to disapproval results in a fear of manipulation or exploitation by others, and a dread of being held in contempt by them. A common cry from parties in mediation is: 'If we give them what they are asking for, they will be laughing all the way to the bank!' We will consider below how these fears translate into behavioural strategies.

Corporate and Community Self-esteem

Self-esteem is not confined to individuals: it can also manifest itself in corporations and other larger groups. An entire country's self-esteem can be lifted when its national football team wins a match or a competition. Corporate self-esteem is also an important factor in commercial disputes. The sense of hurt experienced by a company can be as powerful a driver as it is to an individual: 'Who do they take us for?' 'What sort of a company do they believe they are dealing with?' The dreaded disapproval will be felt vicariously through the sentiments of the executives and other personnel of an organization.

In a community or social context, the need for approval and the aversion to disapproval can occasionally produce extremes of behaviour. For example, the need to maintain the same status as that of our neighbours results in a corresponding concern that the neighbours, and others, will look down upon us, or in some way we will be humiliated, if we do not maintain that status. An illustration of this can be found in issues of honour and face. Take, for example, the extreme phenomenon of 'honour killings', whereby families feel compelled to take the most extreme steps (including homicide) to avoid the shame and dishonour that their offspring might bring upon them. The approval of those around them is so essential to their self-esteem that the disapproval of those 'neighbours' is abhorred. The fear of what these others might think is so strong that it causes behaviour that may generally be regarded by others as extreme. Mediators will be familiar with the situation whereby parties in dispute appear to have sacrificed positions of strength in order to avoid losing face. The saving of face and preservation of honour may take on a greater importance in some cultures, but is nevertheless an illustration of the lengths to which some may go to maintain and protect their self-esteem.

Need to be Valued

Disapproval comes in many forms. Our self-concept often involves a need to be both respected and valued. Disrespect, for example, among street gangs, can be seen as the greatest form of insult. Gangs crave the approval of those in the community around them; yet they are surrounded by the disapproval of the wider public. By creating a hierarchy of respect in a parallel fraternity, they are able to maintain their self-esteem by securing the respect of the gang members and other close peers. Hence, to be 'dissed', in an environment where respect is given a high priority, is particularly damaging to self-esteem, so that any sign of disrespect may provoke an extreme response. Not being valued causes similar offence: we are offended if we are not taken seriously or feel we are taken for granted. Many disputes are fuelled by each party believing themselves to be undervalued by the other. In a family or divorce dispute, for example, the wife may feel unappreciated for her contribution to the home, in bringing up the children and enabling the husband to be the breadwinner; at the same time the husband may feel that insufficient credit has been given to him for his abilities to 'put bread on the table'. In a commercial dispute, a company might believe, for example, that the repeated late delivery of goods demonstrates a lack of respect; whereas the other company views the persistent failure to make timely payments for the goods as an impudence. Each feels treated with a lack of due respect by the other: 'How dare they treat us in this way!' In a partnership situation, the fact that one partner has not been consulted about a decision is a recurrent complaint in partnership disputes: the failure to consult is seen as demeaning, and an attack on self-esteem – irrespective of whether or not the decision ultimately made was good or bad. In *Getting to Yes* (1981: 25) Fisher and Ury give an example of the tenant who believes he is a good tenant because he pays his rent '*whenever* the landlady asks for it', whereas the landlady berates the tenant because 'he never pays the rent *until* she asks for it'. Each perceives an affront by the other. Kenneth Cloke, mediator and Director of the Center for Dispute Resolution in Santa Monica, California, in his talks gives the example of the divorce mediation where the principal complaint by the wife was that her husband always placed his cutlery in the sink rather than straight into the dishwasher. The wife felt taken for granted, asking herself: 'Why is it assumed in this house that I am the one who will always take the cutlery out of the sink and place it in the dishwasher?'

In every one of these and other similar situations, each person on one side of the dispute feels a lack of proper appreciation by the other. Each asks himself or herself: 'Why am I being treated in this fashion? Why is it presumed that I will tolerate this and not object?' Their self-esteem is under attack – and they may suffer an amygdala hijack.

A further essential aspect of self-esteem is the need to be heard. This will be dealt with in greater detail in a later chapter (see Chapter 6) but it is important to mention here, as it is a powerful illustration of self-esteem. It is an existential 'given' that we all share a need for self-expression, and with this comes a corresponding need to be heard. Not being heard is the equivalent of not being valued and appreciated. Those who believe they are not heard will feel undervalued, ignored, misunderstood or misrepresented, and are likely to suffer a loss of self-esteem. As we shall see below, one of our coping mechanisms in such circumstances is to ensure, one way or another, that we are heard. This may range from the simple raising of voices in a quarrel, to more far-reaching tactics such as court action, fighting, or possibly in the most extreme cases, of terrorism.

Coping Mechanisms

From all the foregoing, mediators will be well aware that much of the conduct displayed by parties in mediation is likely to be governed almost entirely by self-esteem. Trainee mediators, for example, are taught to avoid asking questions that might intimate an element of disapproval, as this may be perceived as an attack upon the party's self-esteem. Any hint of criticism or condemnation on the part of the mediator will sound hugely judgmental to those in dispute. It is for this reason that mediators are instructed to avoid 'Why?' questions: these demand an explanation or a justification, and are therefore likely to be interpreted as accusatory. In extreme situations, they might provoke an amygdala hijack, and so jeopardize any prospect of a trusting relationship between mediator and party.

We do not allow our self-esteem to become or remain depressed for any length of time. The mediator will be conscious of the fact that the slightest intimation of manipulation or exploitation by the other party, and their mechanisms to defend their self-esteem come into play. Parties will seek at all costs to avoid humiliation. We adopt a range of strategies to build up and maintain our self-concept, and employ a variety of tactical behaviours to protect it. The object of these coping mechanisms is to restore and regain the 'approval' that we feel we have lost. We want to feel good about ourselves again. In many instances, these strategies are aimed at regaining *control* of the situation, or acquiring 'the upper hand'. In a conversation or argument, we may attempt to secure control by raising our voices. It ensures that we are heard while preventing the other from making their point. The raising of the voice is likely to take place at a moment when we feel we are losing control of the situation – whether it is because we believe our arguments are less than cogent or effective, or because the other party is refusing to listen. In either case, the result of shouting will, at least in the short term, create a perception of power, control and 'winning'.

Similarly, with a walk-out: by walking away or leaving the room, the other party is left totally impotent. This in turn engenders a feeling of power and superiority in the person staging the dramatic exit, while leaving the other weak and helpless. Take the following – autobiographical – example: a family sit down to a pleasant family dinner. A conversation follows that turns into a debate; and then, as often occurs with family occasions, the meal ends in a bitter and vociferous argument. The 14-year-old son abruptly leaves the table and on exiting the room gives his father a V-sign. The father realizes that something has been said to the boy to dent his self-esteem, and that the boy's fierce reaction is merely a coping mechanism to the perceived loss of the argument. It is his only way, as he sees it, of regaining the upper hand and of restoring his self-esteem.

Uncertainty, Transiency and the Need for Control

The need for control, as a constituent element of self-esteem, is derived from the existential concept of how we cope with uncertainty and transiency. According to Heidegger, we are 'thrown' into an uncertain world (*Geworfenheit*). Even death, which is the only certainty, is nevertheless hedged about with a vast array of uncertainties: we do not know when, why or how death will occur. Furthermore, everything is subject to change: the change is constant and this transiency is beyond our control. As Heraclitus, the Greek philosopher (535–475 bc), is quoted by Plato (in *Dialogue*) as saying: 'You cannot step twice into the same river.'

When we try to manage or dictate the manner of change, it creates an element of apprehension. For we can never be sure of the results when things become altered, and in many cases we experience unexpected consequences of these modifications. Our decision-making is thus constantly uncertain, as we cannot definitively predict outcomes. This in turn causes us considerable anxiety. The desire for control therefore becomes a coping mechanism to address such levels of uncertainty and the effects of transiency. Without a degree of control we would not be able to live our daily lives against the backdrop of such uncertainty. Not being in control is uncomfortable, and we experience a significant degree of apprehension in such situations. When circumstances become unpredictable in their outcome, when we are unsure of what is happening, or uncertain where it will lead, we feel a strong sense of unease. Mediators need to appreciate this sense of angst surrounding uncertainty, as it resides both in the parties to the dispute as well as in the mediators themselves. The parties will approach mediation with trepidation and anxiety, concerned because they are not able to predict how the process will run, let alone how it might end. Similarly, the mediator will be troubled by each decision taken, fearful of the uncertainty of the consequences of every judgment call made.

The concept of being 'out of our comfort zone' is another demonstration of our discomfort through not being in control. This expression reflects the fear connected to a lack of control in a particular situation. We rarely enjoy being out of our comfort zone because of the endless uncertainties it creates; and we can only return to our comfort zone by regaining control of the particular environment. Those who have struggled with computers will understand how these machines can provide graphic examples of our dislike of being out of control. When the computer seems to work as if it has a mind of its own, when it 'does things I did not tell it to do', or 'refuses to do what I am telling it to do', we are driven to rage. We might even have a desire to put our fist through the screen, or hurl the entire piece of hardware out of the window – a typical example of an amygdala hijack. The computer, albeit a wholly inanimate object consisting of little more than wires and other metal, seems to be in control. The sense of being out of control affects our self-esteem, and we feel demeaned by it. Worse still is the belief that something or someone else is in control of us. Thus, the fear of our losing control is exacerbated by the notion that, through such loss of control, someone else may *gain* control.

Control and Power

Many political, ethnic, racial and religious disputes are fuelled by the fear that others will gain or be in control – 'they will take over' – and hence the struggle to maintain or restore control. Control provides power, and power delivers control. So 'seizing power' is gaining control. Power, therefore, is inextricably bound up with control. Bernard Mayer, in *The Dynamics of Conflict* (2012), describes power as 'the currency of conflict':

> Power is variously defined as the ability to act, to influence an outcome, to get something to happen, or to overcome resistance … For the purpose of understanding the dynamics of conflict, power may be defined as the ability to get one's needs met and to further one's goals.

(2012: 68)

Power can be seen to be equated with control in a number of circumstances. Where knowledge, expertise, information or data is in the possession of one party and is required by the other disputing party, it can lead to a perception of power and hence control of the situation, and over the dispute. Where resources such as money, time or physical strength or energy reside in one party, they may have a sense of power and control over the other. From a litigant's perspective, the power to inflict pain, suffering and humiliation upon the other party gives rise to a strong feeling of control. The corollary is that when parties believe they have lost control over the dispute, they feel powerless and impotent; and their efforts to regain control are synonymous with regaining power.

In commercial and other mediations, parties often enter the process feeling they have lost some or all control over the subject matter of the dispute. At that point they are 'powerless': they see themselves as having 'failed'; they feel ineffective, feeble and vulnerable. This is demeaning, and their self-esteem will not allow them to remain in that state indefinitely. Their negotiations and coping strategies throughout the mediation process will be shaped so as no longer to feel ineffectual and helpless. Their conduct, therefore, will be aimed at restoring their self-esteem so as to regain power, and to recover control.

Understanding these strategies and recognizing them for what they are can be of enormous benefit. Bullying is a good example. Most organizations – be they schools, universities, offices or other workplaces – boast proudly that they operate a 'zero tolerance' policy towards bullying. The bully is identified, reprimanded and punished. But this rarely transforms the bully instantly into a responsible, decent and civilized member of the community. Often the contrary is true: the bully moves on to bully others, and perhaps elsewhere becomes an abuser or a 'batterer'. Were the bullying perhaps to be understood from a psychological perspective, a different means of dealing with it might be found. One explanation for bullying is that it serves as a coping mechanism for loss of or low self-esteem. The bully derives pleasure from denigrating others, and through putting others down achieves a position of power, secures an element of control and is able to feel superior to them. Bullying is thus utilized to feel 'better about oneself', and thereby restore and maintain self-esteem. So, by enabling the bully to regain an element of self-respect – by allocating a position of responsibility, for example, as a prefect if the bullying is taking place in a school, or a line manager if it occurs in an organization – the problem of self-esteem can be addressed in a more constructive manner. Prejudice, racial or otherwise, may involve similar threads: the ability to look down upon others as inferior provides an opportunity for a sense of superiority, power and control, which in turn feeds into our self-esteem.

The powerful nature of self-esteem in its diverse guises as described above translates itself into a variety of other curious behavioural strategies in a mediation. Some of these will no doubt be familiar to many experienced mediators, and are dealt with in greater detail later (see Chapter 8). The following are some examples of these strategies:

- selecting and arguing over the appropriate venue for the mediation: each party, while acknowledging the need for a neutral venue, will nevertheless hope for a venue where they feel they have greater power and control – the upper hand; at the same time they fear an element of manipulation if the suggestion of a venue emanates from the other side to the dispute

- making the first move: each party is reluctant to 'go first' when making offers or proposals – often not for any sound commercial reason, but for fear of getting it wrong (for example, pitching too high or too low) and thereby 'looking foolish'

- 'keeping cards close to the chest': the fear that disclosure will be used against them for manipulation or exploitation purposes

- having the 'last word': this may often result in the mediator being asked to secure one final small or inconsequential sum or concession out of the other party, immediately prior to settlement. It demonstrates the need to regain control of the dispute, by being seen as having 'won'.

With the knowledge that this often seemingly childlike behaviour is precipitated by a need to protect or maintain self-esteem, the mediator will be able to address it with empathy and understanding, rather than incredulous irritation.

The Golden Bridge

Finally, it is often productive for a mediator to remind parties of the existence of self-esteem in the other side's camp. The knowledge and appreciation that our enemies may also be driven by a need to restore their self-esteem can contribute to a mellowing of hostile attitudes. We can all understand the discomfort of humiliation, and even those who wish it upon their enemies may appreciate that it is unlikely to secure a settlement of the dispute. The mediator will regularly be confronted by a party whose perception of the strength of their case is such as to obviate the need to make any concessions: 'Why should we compromise? If we go to court we are bound to win.' This invariably results in impasse: one side refuses to make any shift in position and rigidly opposes any form of further compromise; the other side is reluctant to be humiliated or to 'have their noses ground into the dust'. It is in such stages of the mediation that a mediator might find it productive to introduce the concept of 'the Golden Bridge' – a notion from the writing of Sun Tzu, the 4th century BC Chinese military strategist, from his treatise *The Art of War*, in which he wrote: 'A wise conquering general is one who builds a Golden Bridge upon which his defeated enemy can retreat.' If the enemy is provided with a dignified exit route from the dispute, it will be able to 'save face', and thereby maintain its self-esteem. If the enemy encounters nothing but shame and dishonour in defeat, it will have little option but to fight: for it is only through fighting that it believes it can regain its self-esteem. The mediator can thus invite the assistance of the first party in building that golden bridge, by furnishing some hint of a concession upon which the other party might seize in order to save face. Often, if there is a true permeating desire to end the conflict, the stronger party will find some component of the dispute, however small, which it feels able to relinquish; and the weaker party will equally be prepared to see in that gesture, however small, the opportunity to depart from the dispute with at least some dignity and self-respect intact.

5

Values, Sedimentations and Polarities

The creation of values and value systems is another of the shared existential givens, which are invariably inter connected and interrelated. Values are linked to uncertainty and in turn are associated with self-esteem. From the existentialist perspective, value systems are created so as to help us navigate through the daily uncertainty and transiency of our existence. They serve to address and overcome the ambiguities caused by these insecurities of living. Values are the principles by which we all live, and which provide us with some boundaries and structure to our everyday lives.

Heidegger's view of authenticity and leading an authentic life involves making our own choices, and he proposes that our value systems are the result of making those choices. We can choose our style and mode of living; and we do so to fulfil our possibilities and realize our potential. We can choose to live honestly and truthfully, or we can find some alternative value system upon which we place even greater worth. Our values are created by us, or alternatively they may be created by others and imposed upon or adopted by us. In either instance, the value system will have been generated because we have found it to serve us well. If, for example, in our formative years we were praised for being loyal, we may develop a value system around loyalty. We will have discovered that being loyal has its benefits for us, and may thereafter hold this as a value that is dear to us. Similarly with any other value, such as tidiness, punctuality, honesty or truthfulness. If we are rewarded for such principled behaviour, we are likely to see it as beneficial. These values then become the matters that we cherish and which we regard as important in the way we conduct our lives. Conversely, we may need to shed values if and when we discover that they no longer serve us well. For example, loyalty may be a powerful and sedimented value; but if a person holding such value were to discover that being loyal could cause harm, then that value might need to be suspended or possibly discarded altogether. Parties in dispute often hold on to values despite their adverse effect – 'it is a matter of principle' (see further below) – and, in such instances, the mediator may need to consider whether a reality check or challenge to these values is appropriate, or alternatively whether it might be counter-productive (see Chapter 9, for reality tests).

Value systems can be created not just by an individual, but also by larger groups. Values, as we have seen with self-esteem, can be identified in national, ethnic and cultural groups. Take, for example, the value related to punctuality. The Germanic and northern European approach to punctuality will be readily recognized: being on time is an imperative to that ethnic cultural group. It is trite to point out that 'trains run on time'; meetings and symposiums start at the exact time they are scheduled to start, 'not a minute sooner or a minute later'.

Those who have given conference presentations in these countries may have noted that almost all auditoria will have a clock on the wall, or indeed one clock on each of the four walls. Speakers at such conferences are often subjected to the most rigorous timekeeping for their presentations, occasionally with 'traffic light' signals on the podium going from green to amber to red, to mark the end of their time slot – and occasionally having the microphone switched off after the red light has shown. The Latin or southern European attitude to punctuality, on the other hand, is renowned for its opposite outlook: conferences and meetings are rarely expected to start on time, timetables and schedules are often unreliable, and lateness or lack of punctuality is seldom regarded as a sign of disrespect. Similar ethnic, cultural and geographical disparities can be seen in relation to a wide variety of values, such as honour and face, modesty, loyalty, valour and many others. It is these distinct value systems that make up the small percentage points of difference in human beings; for though we share the existential givens, it is how we respond to them and the way in which we cope with them that render us different from each other. Our responses and our coping strategies are in turn governed by our values and value systems. It is therefore vital for an effective mediator to understand these value systems, in order to be able better to work with them, rather than against them.

Sedimentations

Frequently values and value systems become 'sedimented' – in other words, they become so rigid as to be impervious to rationalization.

Sedimentation, say Strasser and Strasser, is a term used by existentialists influenced by phenomenologists such as Merleau-Ponty to describe:

> ... the way human beings become stuck or fixed in certain beliefs and behaviour patterns that deposit themselves deep down in our belief systems in a similar fashion to the sediment that sinks to the bottom of a liquid. These values, assumptions about living and behaviour patterns become integrated to such a degree in the way we operate on a daily basis that they become 'sedimented' and appear immovable.
>
> (Strasser and Strasser, 1997: 90)

People with such sedimented values may be entirely unaware that they possess them, and may go through their lives without knowing how sedimented they appear to others; alternatively, they may believe that such inflexibility in their value system is entirely normal. A colleague tells the story of a family holiday, when they visited another family abroad. The two families, and particularly the husbands, had been good friends for many years. One afternoon, the visiting husband poured himself a glass of wine from a bottle in the fridge, and noticed that all the wine and beer bottles were stacked in the fridge with their labels facing outwards. When he replaced the bottle of wine he inadvertently failed to ensure that the label was facing outwards. His friend was extremely annoyed, taking such omission as a personal affront. His sedimentation referred to a value around tidiness and 'order', and he was quite impervious to the fact that this value had become so 'irrational' and rigidly sedimented as to now jeopardize a lifelong friendship. In these circumstances it would have been entirely counter-productive for the colleague to try to persuade the husband that it was only a minor transgression, and that it should be of little consequence in the greater scheme of things.

Such sedimented values are not uncommon and are encountered in a variety of conflict situations. In workplace disputes, for example, sedimented values such as punctuality and tidiness are a typical source of contention. If punctuality ranks highly in the order of values held by an employer, then an employee who is unpunctual, even by a small margin, will be perceived as both disrespectful to the organization and personally insulting to the employer. It will serve no useful purpose to point out to the employer that being only a minute late should not be looked upon so severely, and that other qualities, such as loyalty, diligence, industriousness and conscientiousness, should be given greater weight. Similarly with tidiness in the workplace: to a line manager with a sedimented value system related to tidiness, the worker with an untidy desk or a cluttered room is seen as worthless: a 'problem' or a 'liability'. Such an employee will be identified as detracting from the overall productivity of the company. It is entirely irrelevant that he or she may be hardworking, creative and resourceful: the sedimented value renders the line manager blind to such qualities.

It is the strict adherence to sedimented values that often drives parties into conflict, and also prevents them from reaching a resolution: 'This is a matter of principle,' say the parties, seeking to justify their rigidly entrenched positions. 'Principles are a costly luxury,' retort their advisers lamely. But it is precisely when the parties stand firm 'on principle' that the mediator needs to understand and work closely with the values so as to secure that vital shift of attitude necessary for a satisfactory resolution. These are the occasions when non-judgmental acceptance is required on the part of the mediator. If the mediator were to challenge the expressed inflexible value, the party would expend time and energy seeking to persuade the mediator of its reasonableness – and would through that effort become even more deeply embedded in his view (see further on non-judgmental acceptance, Chapter 6). By accepting the sedimentation without criticism or condemnation, the mediator avoids further entrenchment by the party, and enables the party to move on.

Polarities

Conflict inevitably brings with it polarities. In psychological terms, polarities manifest themselves each time we make a choice: when we say 'yes' to something, we are inevitably saying 'no' to something else. When we choose a value as being something that we perceive to be good for us, we are simultaneously rejecting another value that we deem to be bad. So, for example, if we regard honesty as a value to revere, we are at the same time categorizing dishonesty as something we find repugnant. Similarly, in the above examples, where tidiness and punctuality are celebrated as beneficial values, untidiness and lack of punctuality will automatically become polarized as harmful. Recognizing these polarities when they are presented by parties in a mediation will enable a mediator to understand the reason for an impasse: one party 'sticks' strongly to a belief, because it abhors the contrary belief held by the other party – and scorns the other party for holding it.

It might appear from the above that polarities are invariably seen as denoting opposites. In physics, magnetic polarity involves opposite poles – north and south – and they also present a further concept: that of attraction and repulsion. Like poles attract and opposite poles repel. Electrical circuits similarly have positive and negative poles, where the electric current flows in opposite directions. Yet psychological polarities need not necessarily be direct or extreme opposites: something may be good, and the other thing merely less good; and while honesty may be of critical importance, being 'economical with the truth' or not *entirely* honest may simply be less acceptable.

Parties in dispute nevertheless often describe themselves as diametrically opposite: being 'poles apart'. They will perceive themselves as holding values significantly contradictory to those held by the parties on the other side of the dispute. In *Existential Counselling in Practice*, Emmy van Deurzen-Smith described this in the following way (as cited by Strasser and Strasser):

> What stands out as a basic principle is that human existence is a struggle between opposites. There are two sides to every experience. Each argument has a counter argument. Positive aspects turn out to have negative counter parts and vice versa. People always find themselves somewhere on the continuum between life and death, good and bad, positive and negative, active and passive, happiness and sadness, closeness and distance.
>
> (Deurzen-Smith, 1988: 58)

We appreciate polarities, however, because they provide clear and definable boundaries: we prefer things to be black and white rather than grey; we like to consider matters in terms of their polarities, such as good and bad; strong and weak; constructive and obstructive; order and chaos. The importance to the mediator of understanding values and polarities is that they help the mediator, and the party themselves, to isolate the issues which they each see as critically important, and those which each may consider to be immaterial or of lesser significance. These polarities can thus pinpoint the boundaries for negotiation and mediation, helping to reveal 'bottom lines' or the 'red lines' which can and cannot be crossed.

Ambiguities

Polarities may also reveal a party's ambiguities: 'I want to settle, but I am not prepared to apologize'; 'I believe in honesty but I do not wish to reveal to the other party my weaknesses'. The mediator can sometimes assist by highlighting a party's ambiguities and so raise their own awareness of these contradictions: 'On the one hand I can sense that you believe in being steadfast and resolute, and you fear that changing your mind might appear as a sign of weakness; and yet on the other hand you appreciate that in order to resolve the dispute you may need to be more flexible.' The mediator thus conveys an understanding of the fact that being unbending and 'firm of purpose' is an important principle to that party; but at the same time, the mediator shines a spotlight on the polarity of that principle, namely that being less *in*flexible and occasionally changing one's mind might possibly lead to a resolution.

Understanding these values and their polarities will therefore be instrumental in assisting each party to devise a formula for settlement that will accord, not only with their own principles and value systems, but also with those of the other party.

A further example of the usefulness of realizing a person's values and polarities may be illustrated by the following vignette. Two colleagues on a business trip abroad make an excursion to the local bazaar in search of gifts to bring home to their respective wives. They both purchase attractive cashmere scarves. One indicates that in order to ensure that his wife fully appreciates the gift he will need to remove the scarf from its plain brown paper packaging and place it in an Hermès or Harrods bag before giving it to her. The other colleague indicates that he would need to do the opposite: if the scarf were in a smart, expensively branded bag or wrapping, he would need to transfer it to an ordinary brown paper wrapping, as his wife would be annoyed at the thought of his paying an unduly high price for it. In this example, one person has a value system in which status, prestige and reputation are prominent. The other is concerned with frugality and thrift. A mediator will often encounter such values in a commercial mediation and it may be vital to identify them correctly: if one party is concerned only with reputation and the other only with money, the mediator's approach will need to be tailored to each in a slightly different way. But once these values are detected and recognized, the mediator can more effectively manage the issues and work on the potential outcomes in the dispute. There would be little point in striving towards a solution involving the preservation of status and reputation if that mattered little or not at all to that party; equally, it would be ineffectual to concentrate on a financial solution if it fell short of addressing the party's value system associated with status and reputation.

It is when values, and particularly those which are held most dear, are challenged, confronted or abused by others that emotions are aroused, and conflict becomes inevitable and intractable. The level of emotion created by these value systems and their polarities will vary from person to person. What may anger one party may leave another totally unmoved. This is likely to be the result of each party holding differing values and beliefs. If the attack is upon values which are not strongly held, the party will be less troubled by an incursion upon them. If, for example, one person's sedimented value system attaches undue weight to modesty, they will find exhibitionism utterly vulgar; whereas to another such attention-seeking might be inconsequential. And as we have seen, if punctuality is a sedimented value then we will naturally be offended if the other is consistently late; whereas persistent lateness may have no effect upon someone whose belief system views punctuality as an irrelevance. Thus values are fundamental to our self-esteem and lie at the heart of most conflicts.

Shared values, on the other hand, can be a useful concept for a mediator to utilize in order to reduce the effect of polarization, and to secure an attitude shift. We have seen in Chapter 2 how a mediator may assist the parties by highlighting their common aims and objectives. When parties in a dispute are made to recognize that the dispute throws up values that are common to both of them, and that they share, it can have a beneficial effect upon those holding entrenched and polarized positions. Parties will often share values such as loyalty, honesty and integrity, but simply view their own attitudes towards these values as more authentic and appropriate than those of the other. For example, business executives in a bitter partnership dispute may each have a passionate desire to secure the success or survival of a business. If they are able to appreciate that the dispute has arisen because they both share a strong value, that of loyalty to the business, their personal animosity towards each other may be diminished: they may then see that they merely have opposing views as to how their values can be realized. Similarly, the hostility of warring parents towards each other in a divorce may be tempered if they are able to grasp the fact that they have identical values surrounding their children. If they were able to accept that they simply cannot agree as to how those values may be actualized, they might more readily moderate their hostility towards each other. In this way, the mediator can succeed in reducing the dispute from a fiercely antagonistic battle to a mere difference of opinion.

A further illustration of the benefit of common values can be seen in the following example. Two people with unfriendly and antagonistic views of one another discover that they both support the same football team – or share a taste for the same genre of music; like the same books or enjoy the same plays; or enjoy travelling to the same places. Their perceptions of each other can radically and instantly change. The realization that there are common attributes between them and that they have shared values can bring about a rapprochement, a narrowing of the perceived gap between them, and so remove or diminish the hostility that previously existed between them. The commonalities in values serve to reduce the level of conflict. In all the above situations, an understanding of the parties' respective value systems and their polarities will assist the mediator in guiding the parties towards such realizations themselves as to their mutual unities. A proper appreciation of the values presented by the parties will also enable the mediator to establish whether, and if so how, it may be productive or unproductive to work with the values, rather than attempt to challenge them. If the values are so sedimented as to be impossible to change, there may be little useful purpose in confronting them. On the other hand, a little gentle 'stirring' may assist in altering some hitherto deeply rooted perceptions. In either case, the mediator might do well to heed the advice given at many UK railway stations: do not leave baggage unattended.

6

Interpersonal Relationships and the Need to be Heard

It is an existential given that we all share a need for self-expression. With that need comes a corresponding desire to create interpersonal relationships. These are yet again coping mechanisms we adopt to address the uncertainties of our existence in an uncertain, temporal and transient world. From a mediator's point of view, conflict is relational: it always centres upon relationships; without a relationship there would be no dispute. There are, of course, *intra*-personal conflicts in which no external person is engaged, but it would be a conflict that a psychotherapist or psychiatrist, rather than a mediator, is called upon to resolve. Disputes evolve from something that has occurred within a relationship between people, and as such are usually potentially destructive of that association or liaison. In most cases, the relationship has arisen out of choice: although we cannot choose our relatives, we generally choose our friends, our contracting partners, and most of those with whom we wish to interact, whether in a commercial context or socially. This fact may exacerbate the psychological elements of the conflict. For the greater the degree of 'connectedness', the more intense are the emotional constituents of the dispute. The 20th century American sociologist Louis Coser observed that the closer the relationship, the more passionate the conflict. This may be a reassuring factor for many warring matrimonial couples as well as troubled parents and offspring. A relationship in which the parties are overly fearful of conflict between them may be evidence of the *fragility* of that relationship: neither party has the confidence to express their views freely for fear of damaging or destroying the bond. Where, on the other hand, the parties feel able to criticize or insult each other, express anger and fury, and even verbally abuse each other without undue concern that the relationship will end as a result, it may in fact demonstrate a strength in the relationship. Hence, when a child says: 'I hate you, Mummy!', or: 'I wish you were dead!', it reveals a powerful confidence in the strength of the affiliation, enabling the child to express itself without fear of irretrievably destroying the attachment it has to its mother.

We are more intensely affected by the actions and words of those we love – and whose love is important to us – than by the sentiments or behaviour of those about whom we have little or no feeling. Similarly, a conflict between those whose mutual approval is important is likely to be more severe than a dispute with people whose opinions are irrelevant. This is especially so where we have selected those parties ourselves, so we may feel a greater degree of responsibility for the potential breakdown of the relationship.

In many instances there will be an ultimate need or desire to restore and maintain those relationships. In a commercial context, organizations may benefit from a degree of cooperation in order to thrive and make profit. The existence of a dispute among profit-oriented organizations is commercially indefensible, as it depletes them of the valuable commodities of time, energy, money and productivity. In these instances, the mediator's role is to manage that dispute so that the relationship is either restored to the mutual satisfaction of the parties, or, alternatively, terminated so that the parties may go their separate ways without the bitterly destructive elements that are often associated with such endings. In other settings, the need for collaboration is more vital: in small communities, for example, where people are dependent upon each other for their very existence, they could not survive without their neighbours' cooperation and collaboration. Here, conflict resolution has a greater urgency. In Central Africa, for example, ethnic communities have been known to resolve their differences 'around a campfire', despite each having suffered atrocities at the hands of the other. This is a result of the scarcity of resources, which often creates a more critical need to cooperate with each other.

Heidegger's approach to our relatedness was considered briefly in Chapter 1. In *Sein und Zeit* he approached the essence of our existence as '*Dasein*', or 'being there', viewing our existence as it is in relation to the rest of the world. We do not and cannot exist in isolation; from the moment we are born and 'thrown' into the world to the moment we die we are always in relationship to and with others. Even when we are entirely alone, our solitude must be viewed as relational: we are alone because of our separation from others. For Sartre, our interpersonal relationships and our relatedness to one another is a principal cause of conflict. It is an impediment to the fulfilment of the aspirations of our existence: 'Hell is other people'.

We have also noted (see Chapter 1), in *Being and Nothingness*, that Sartre considered how we define ourselves through the judgments and observations ('*le regard*') of others.

The creation of relationships cannot be isolated from our need for self-expression. This is most aptly demonstrated by our creation of interpersonal relationships through social interaction on the World Wide Web. The growth of social media has resulted in a constant flow of self-expression. We speak, text and email incessantly on mobile telephones; we pursue relationships by following others on Twitter and crave that they follow us; we use Facebook to exchange messages, share photos and videos; we post and constantly update our profiles so that, according to the website, we can 'connect and share with the people in our lives'; and we use social media platforms such as LinkedIn as a business-oriented social networking service.

The Need to be Heard

The desire to express ourselves has a corresponding need: the need to be heard. It is plainly futile to express ourselves if no one is listening. In *Existentialism: An Introduction, Guide and Assessment*, John Macquarrie refers to the views of Martin Buber, the Austrian-born Israeli philosopher whom he describes as one of the 'pioneers in the investigation of interpersonal relations' (1972: 16). He makes the following interpretation of one aspect of Buber's work:

> Very characteristic of Buber's thought is his use of the word *dialogue*. To say that the interpersonal relation is dialogical is to insist on that 'mutual' character already mentioned … A genuine

relation to another person cannot be one-sided, dominating, or possessive; it must consist of openness and willingness to listen and receive as well as speak and to give.

(1972: 109)

The desire to be heard is not merely a wish to be listened to, but also a craving to be understood, and – ideally – to be agreed with and vindicated. In *Getting to Yes*, Roger Fisher and William Ury put it in this way:

People listen better if they feel that you have understood them. They tend to think that those who understand them are intelligent and sympathetic people whose own opinions may be worth listening to. So if you want the other side to appreciate *your* interests, begin by demonstrating that you appreciate *theirs*.

(1981: 52)

This again emanates from the concept of self-esteem and our need for approval. We enjoy speaking to those who agree with us; we take pleasure in blogging and we place posts on the internet in the anticipation that others will 'like' what we say and agree with and approve of it. We would be less inclined to speak to those from whom we anticipate nothing but criticism. This would naturally be damaging to our self-esteem. As previously stated, we like to think well of ourselves and therefore it is important that others think well of us.

Complaint Handling

Almost as damaging to our self-esteem as the lack of approval is the sense of not being heard at all. In a culture and environment where freedom of speech is placed on a pedestal, the absence of a voice can be devastating. Protest marches and graffiti may both be seen as an example of people exercising their need to have a voice and their desire to be heard, when perhaps their voice is not being heard in other quarters. Many disputes are triggered or prolonged as a result of parties feeling they have not been listened to, properly or at all. This causes them to feel ignored and hence undervalued and unappreciated. The escalation of consumer complaints is an example of the effect of parties not feeling properly heard. The complaint-handling industry has a regrettably poor record of dealing with and responding effectively to complaints. This is usually the result of an unfortunate failure to understand the psychological needs of the complainant. The 'average' complainant wants to be listened to and to be taken seriously; they want appreciation, some understanding, empathy or sympathy; and, ultimately, they would like to be proved right. Often, they do not even wish to be seen as someone who makes a complaint, for fear of the disapproval that this will generate. So it naturally enhances the self-esteem of all complainants if they are seen as being reasonable in raising an issue or are deemed justified in making the complaint. This, they hope, will then precipitate some appropriate action.

In many instances the person handling the complaint is unable – or not authorized – to provide what the complainant is really seeking. The complaint may be entirely without foundation; the complainant's demand may be wholly disproportionate; or the complaint handler may simply not be in a position or authorized to respond adequately. However, the manner in which the response to the complaint is made, and the way in which unpalatable messages are conveyed, will almost certainly govern whether or not the complaint escalates further. In some cases, the complaint starts out as being little other than critical but constructively intended feedback; it may be a mere expression of dissatisfaction. But when such feedback is poorly handled, and the complainant is left feeling unappreciated and undervalued, it can quickly cause the feedback to escalate into a complaint and to spiral out of control, culminating in bitter and prolonged litigation.

A poor or ineffective complaint handler tends to adopt a protective attitude, often appearing to be 'defending the indefensible'. Even worse, they may, inadvertently or otherwise, imply some level of criticism towards the complainant. When this is interpreted as suggesting that the complainant is at fault or that they themselves may in some way be responsible for the problem, the situation can be aggravated beyond control. The difficulty often lies in the fact that persons handling complaints carry on their shoulders the corporate self-esteem and reputation of the organization they are trying to protect. And they will additionally need to cope with their own self-esteem: they will have an eye over their shoulder, craving the approval of their superiors by successfully resolving, deflecting or 'batting away' as many complaints as possible. All this leads, predictably, to defensive positions, resulting in a clash of values, perceptions and self-esteem.

Non-judgmental Acceptance

One means of avoiding such clash of positions, whether in handling complaints or in disputes in general, is to adopt an approach of 'non-judgmental acceptance'. This is a vital tool in the mediator's tool box, and involves the mediator accepting a party's position at their own valuation, without challenge or question, however extreme or irrational that position may be. Such 'acceptance' does not involve agreeing with that party's position, but is merely an acceptance of a differing view without critical analysis. By being non-judgmental in the face of extreme, or even disagreeable, positions, the mediator can avoid confrontation, and so can divert the hostility that would inevitably follow a challenge. For if the mediator were to contest or in some way question the party's extreme position, the mediator would simply become another 'enemy', another person in the long line of people 'who do not understand'. Contesting extreme positions can also have a wholly counter-productive effect: the party will be driven to devoting their energy and time persuading the mediator of the validity of their extreme position. Thus, instead of engaging in a more positive frame of mind and concentrating on a solution to the problem, they squander time and energy dwelling upon and defending their stance, which may be the cause of the dispute. What might initially have been expressed merely as an exaggerated view is thus converted into a firmly held and deeply entrenched stance, merely through seeking to justify it. Take the example of a party who announces to the mediator that they do not trust lawyers because 'all lawyers are crooks, merely after your money'. The natural reaction of a mediator might be to raise an eyebrow, and possibly vocally challenge such an apparent exaggeration. The result of such an intervention is that the party then feels obliged to justify their statement. They may then spend the ensuing period seeking to persuade the mediator of the correctness of their view. By the end of that period, they would be more firmly convinced of their position (that lawyers are disreputable and unethical) than when they first made their assertion. Furthermore, the mediator, through his or her challenge, is likely to have jeopardized the prospects of building rapport and promoting a trusting relationship – so critically important particularly in the early stages of any mediation. Confronting one person's robust stance with an opposite robust opinion leads to a pointless cycle of positional antagonism. Brute force met with brute force results only in a violent clash. The futility of such skirmishes is well recognized in martial arts. Fisher and Ury describe it in this way:

> As in the Oriental martial arts of judo and jujitsu, avoid pitting your strength against theirs directly; instead use your skill to step aside and turn their strength to your ends. Rather than resisting force, channel it into exploring interests, inventing options for mutual gain, and searching for independent standards.
>
> (1981: 114)

Non-judgmental acceptance thus promotes a more fluid response to rigid positions. By refraining from pitting one position against another, and by avoiding a cycle of attack, defence and counter-attack, we avoid any threat to self-esteem. We create a 'safe' environment that can allow a party freely to express their worldview and to feel truly heard. By listening without judgment, we enable defences and guards to be dropped, and we allow the parties to reveal their values and their value systems with greater transparency. In turn, they will also expose their own ambiguities and vulnerabilities. Without such listening, complaints, disagreements and quarrels intensify, and mere differences of opinion escalate into acrimonious disputes. The far-reaching consequences of not being heard are all too common: 'They are not listening, so I have no alternative but to fight (whether with armies of lawyers in court, or legions of soldiers on the battlefield) – that will make them listen.'

It is for these reasons that the skills of 'active' listening are such vital tools in the mediator's or complaint-handler's tool box. Until parties feel truly heard they are in no place or frame of mind to listen to others, let alone to listen to reason. It is only once they feel they have been truly heard and understood that the parties are on a platform where they are amenable to a shift of their rigid position. So when parties believe they have not hitherto been heard, it is very effective for the mediator to demonstrate that at least he or she is really listening, appreciating their position and understanding. This can sometimes defuse much of the anger and emotion directed by one party against the other. By deploying the communication skills referred to in Chapter 2, such as reflecting back, paraphrasing and summarizing, the mediator can most effectively *prove* to a party beyond doubt that they have been truly heard and that they are truly being listened to by the mediator. The mediator thus listens in a wholly *altruistic* manner – not for the benefit of themselves as mediators in order to ascertain facts – but almost entirely for the party, to allow them a platform from which to make their voice heard. In this way and without undue effort, a party's need to be listened to and valued can easily be addressed. By investing a little time in 'active listening', the mediator can demonstrate to the parties not only that they have been heard, but that they have also been understood and accepted without judgment. And, once heard, the party is disarmed, their emotions subside and points of resistance are removed; the party's anger is assuaged and there is nothing more against which to rail. Their self-esteem is restored.

7

Perceptions, Assumptions and Biases

The single and most essential aim of a mediator, as identified in Chapter 2, is that of securing a perception shift in the parties to the conflict. It is this shift that may produce the vital change in attitude needed to bring about a narrowing of the gap between opposing factions. Without such a change, the parties remain fixed in their obstructive outlook and their unproductive views, of each other and of the dispute.

Perceptions are the assumptions that we make about the world around us in order to bring some sense and certainty to our existence. They are unique, in that no one else will experience the same perception, nor will they have the same perception at any two different times. The formulation of our assumptions is, once again, our coping mechanism for navigating an uncertain and transient world. Perceptions help our understanding of what we see and hear and feel: they are the interpretations we form in order to gain an understanding of the objects, people and facts that populate our world. Nietzsche famously stated: 'There are no facts, only interpretations.' Kierkegaard, like Nietzsche, proposed that objective truth is little more than a perception, and that the paradox lies in the objective uncertainty of the truth. Husserl also argued that objects were not objects in themselves, but only objects in terms of our subjective experiences of them; consequently, all existence is merely a subjective interpretation of being.

What we consider to be our 'knowledge' is made up of a wealth of perceptions and assumptions. When a party says: 'I know what they are like and I know what they are capable of', this so-called knowledge will be the accumulation of a series of interpretations, in turn based upon a whole library of assumptions and observations. These are likely to be an historical reflection of our past experiences. For example, a man walks into a room wearing a suit: we will immediately make a number of assumptions about him based upon our past experiences of men in suits. If our previous experience of men in suits is confined to lawyers, we are likely to make an assumption that the man is a lawyer. If we have had certain experiences connected with lawyers, we may add those experiences to our assumptions. A curious example of such perceptions influenced by assumptions can be seen in the effect of the industrial tribunals in the UK in the mid-1960s. These were quasi-courts formed to deal with bitter employment disputes, particularly those involving trade unions who were then seen to be flexing powerful muscles. The judges sitting in the tribunals were among the most senior of the judiciary at the time, but they sat in the tribunal not wearing horsehair wigs and crimson gowns, but ordinary business suits. Many attribute the failure of these tribunals – they were changed to employment tribunals in the late

1990s – to the fact that the absence of wigs and gowns detracted from the authoritative weight of the court and of the distinctive eminence of those passing judgments and making decisions. The parties coming to the tribunal, and particularly the trade unions, had a different perception of the panel sitting in judgment because they wore only business suits, and hence they had less respect for their decisions. It was said that the parties failed to attribute to the tribunal the same gravitas as they might have to a court, based upon their assumptions, acquired from past experiences, about judges in wigs and gowns. Consequently, the decisions and judgments of the tribunal were treated with less respect than if they had been made and delivered by judges in traditional dress.

Thus our perceptions will involve an element of expectation: What do I expect from what I observe or have heard, based on my previous experience? An example of the strength of such assumptions can be seen in the following conundrum: 'A father and son are involved in a road traffic accident. The father unfortunately dies at the scene, but the son is taken to hospital. The surgeon takes one look at the boy and says: "I cannot operate on him: he is my son."'

To many, this will appear to be a non sequitur – an impossible statement to make. That is because the assumption and expectation, based upon past experience or biases, is that the surgeon is male; whereas if the surgeon were female, and hence the boy's *mother*, the statement would make perfect sense.

As Ernesto Spinelli describes it in *The Interpreted World*: 'One interpretive variable in perception based upon past experience is our *expectation* of what to perceive. This phenomenon is often referred to as the *perceptual set*' (2005: 46).

Such expectations can sometimes have a negative influence: a person who has been struck by lightning will be anxious about being struck again, whereas someone who has never been a victim of a lightning strike is unlikely to have any such concern. This can readily translate into dispute situations, where a party who is a victim of an injustice may more readily suspect that further injustice is likely to be occasioned.

Spinelli expands on this:

… in the area of person perception we are not content with simply seeing and noting the physical characteristics of others. Instead we go beyond these obvious features and infer their underlying motives, interests, personality traits, psychological state, fears, social status, thoughts, and so on.

(2005: 59)

The above is a good vindication of Husserl's approach, that 'objects are not objects in themselves, but only objects in terms of our subjective experiences of them'.

Perceptions are assumptions that we all make – about the people we meet, their appearance, their intellect, their behaviour, and, most importantly in disputes, their motivations. In fact, the issues actually under consideration here are *mis*perceptions. For invariably these assumptions are incorrect and are founded upon a mistaken assumption about the conduct or motivations of another. When allowed to fester for any period of time, such misperceptions can become fixed in the mind as established facts. The more tenuous the relationship, the less prospect there is of one party giving the other the benefit of the doubt. And so parties proceed deeper into conflict, harbouring grudges based upon perceptions and assumptions created historically and reinforced over periods of weeks, months or even years. Thus one company may make sinister assumptions as to why a supplier was continually late in delivering goods: 'They are trying to put us out of business.' In another case a family member will harbour a lifelong grudge against a family member because 'they never came to Granny's funeral'; or an executive will smart in the belief that his wife 'was snubbed by the sales director at the office party'. These assumptions will often be far from the truth.

Emails are also notorious for creating misperceptions, as people will read into them tones of voice and meanings which simply do not exist, or are wholly unintentional. For example, consider emails that start simply with the name of the other person: 'Michael' rather than 'Dear Michael …', or 'John' instead of 'Hi John' or 'Good Morning John'. These may be interpreted as being written in anger because we associate being addressed in this way by someone – a parent, or a spouse, or an employer – shouting at us when they are angry. We thus tend to infer an added exclamation mark to the end of the name, and hear their voice raised.

It is therefore hardly surprising that parties in dispute have a distorted or jaundiced view of the persons on the other side of the conflict, when they base their perceptions upon past experiences. Those who have suffered a severe injustice at the hands of another are likely to view that other in the light of that injustice. If they believe the other party to be a villain, charlatan, fraudster or cheat, they may therefore interpret and judge all their subsequent words and actions in the light of the standards of a villain, charlatan, fraudster or cheat. They will be sceptical, if not cynical, in their inferences as to the other party's motives, and may impute ulterior motives based simply upon their earlier bad experience. To the psychologically uninformed mediator or to any objective onlooker, this may even appear as a form of paranoia, but to the party involved their perception will be a valid truth. This highlights two important features in all aspects of conflict management and conflict resolution: first, that the perceptions held by each party will be passionately viewed as the only real objective truth; and secondly, that the mediator's task is to assist in dispelling those misperceptions and wrongful assumptions in order to have any prospect of securing a rapprochement towards settlement. Mediators are ideally placed to effect such a change: they are frequently privy to the perceptions of both parties, often simultaneously, and so are able to grasp immediately where the mismatch lies and perhaps even how the disparity has arisen. By dispelling even the most marginal misunderstanding, the mediator can help to narrow the gap between the contesting parties.

In Chapter 2 the difficulties facing a mediator in securing such a shift in perception were discussed. Long-held views about the subject matter of the dispute, as well as about the persons involved, lead to rigid sedimentations. The entrenchment is often fuelled by the polarization effect of the conflict: parties attract and gather around themselves those who are like-minded and support their outlook. Those polarized in this way align themselves with one or other of the parties; they do so because they are likely to have adopted, or to have been robustly influenced by, the assumptions and biases of the party they support. When this takes place on both sides of the conflict, it tends to encourage the drawing of opposing battle lines. These are the hardened attitudes of the parties that the mediator will need to change, and within minutes rather than weeks, months or years. A mediator can use the mediation process as an excellent forum for identifying, addressing and confronting these assumptions and misperceptions, and then help parties to dispel them.

Cognitive Biases

Our perceptions and assumptions are inevitably influenced by our prejudices and biases. These biases will in turn have been created as a result of our own past experiences, or adopted from what we have heard or seen in others. They may result from social, economic or ethnic identification, because we tend to categorize ourselves into groups. In so doing we immediately differentiate ourselves from other groups, and this can result in polarization and the 'Us and Them' experience, as in Sartre's proposition of 'the Other'. The views we hold of 'the Other' can become representational biases: they are built upon what it is that these people represent to us, reflecting in turn our previous experiences: 'Southern Europeans are much more emotional than northern Europeans.' We thus create our own subjective social truths, as proposed by Kierkegaard, and these then become our reality.

Take, for example, the spectator at a football match who observes an incident on the pitch that is deemed by the referee to be a foul. The spectator's perception of the truth of the incident will depend upon which team's player is alleged to have committed the foul: if by a member of the team that the spectator supports, no foul will have been seen. If by the opposing team player, it will have been seen as the most flagrant and heinous offence. Such disparate views will be held on both sides. Another example can be found in the circumstances of a road traffic offence, when divergent perceptions are adopted and legitimized by the courts. A motorist drives across a traffic signal at red, an act that would invariably be seen as a relatively minor misdemeanour, and one with which many drivers might have some sympathy. Were that motorist, however, to cross the traffic signal at red and collide with another car, killing all its occupants, the perceptions of that driver's behaviour are likely to be very different – both by the courts and by the public. Yet the 'criminal' conduct – or in legal parlance, the *actus reus* – is identical, and only the consequence is different. The driver has no control over whether another car is crossing the intersection at the same time, or whether it is carrying a young family.

Many biases are a form of irrational deviation in our judgment, and will often lack logical reasoning. Our self-esteem, however, will not allow us to concede that these prejudicial inferences we make about others and about objects and issues are made up of irrational distortions and inaccuracies. We may not even admit that such perceptions exist at all. As a result, our self-esteem, and our fear of disapproval by others, obliges us to disguise these prejudices and cloak them with respectability. We convince ourselves that they are not illogical but are in fact matters of 'common sense'; that they 'stand to reason'; that they are the result of 'educated guesses'; and we are happy to 'jump on the bandwagon'; or to rely upon stereotyping as proof that our intuition is infallible. Similarly we seek out evidence that supports our perception and we disregard evidence to the contrary. If, for example, we have taken an instant and irrational dislike to someone, we will take pleasure in discovering some fact about them that vindicates our view: 'I knew he could not be trusted.' At the same time we will ignore a host of evidence that might prove us wrong. This is often described as *confirmation bias*. It is frequently observed in the context of litigation, where it is not uncommon for lawyers to appear to disregard evidence that tends to weaken or contradict their client's case; moreover, they seem to accumulate a deepening conviction about the strength of their client's case immediately after proceedings are issued. Lawyers understandably wish to reassure themselves of the correctness of their position once they have made an irrevocable commitment to their client's cause. Thereafter, as they build a fortress around their client's evidence, they become increasingly supportive of their client's position, growing less objective and more biased as their commitment deepens.

> They [litigators] feel the need to resolve internal dissonance as they prepare for scheduled adjudications. They often eliminate all of the self-doubts they experienced when they first accepted the cases. As they become prepared for trial, they no longer entertain uncertainties concerning the rights of their clients to prevail ... As these individuals become more convinced of the certainty of their impending 'victories', they lose all perspective regarding the objective strengths and weaknesses of their case.
>
> (Craver, 2005: 371)

The litigator's self-esteem will not permit the belief that they may have backed the wrong horse and that their client's case is weaker than they initially advised. Conversely, if they begin to fear a possible failure of their case, they may convince themselves that they will lose, so as to avoid the ignominy of disappointment when the ultimate judgment is delivered. It is a similar phenomenon when we make 'post-purchase rationalizations': convincing ourselves that we made the right decision, thereby dispelling any sense of doubt we may entertain about the process. Yet again, the root of such behaviour is self-esteem.

Prejudices, by the very fact of their irrational nature, present us with ambiguities and contradictions. We would prefer to think of ourselves as rational and consistent beings: internal inconsistency is seen as a weakness or fault. So we are uncomfortable when confronted with evidence that conflicts with our beliefs. This discomfort is often described as *cognitive dissonance*. We address our dissonance by seeking to reduce or eliminate it: we place greater weight upon facts and matters that support our views, and discount all other matters that conflict with them. Some might regard this as putting our heads ostrich-like in the sand. Yet we will be convinced of our subjective truths.

Leon Festinger, the American social psychologist who first advanced the theory of cognitive dissonance, gives the following example in his book, written with Riecken and Schachter, *When Prophecy Fails* (1956: 28). A cult prophesied a UFO landing on a particular day, and that the destruction of the Earth would follow. When the prophecy failed and nothing occurred, the members of the cult refused to believe that their faith in the prediction had been misplaced. They chose, rather, to believe that the Earth had been given 'a second chance', and that they could nevertheless continue zealously to convert others. The result was that the numbers of the cult increased dramatically afterwards.

We can find many examples of our attempts at the rationalization of irrational biases. Upon placing a bet on a horse, the gambler becomes increasingly firmly convinced that the selected horse will win. Conversely, they may convince themselves that the horse will fall at the first fence, so as to ensure they do not feel quite so bad about themselves when the horse fails to win. The expression 'sour grapes', taken from Aesop's fable the Fox and the Grapes, describes the situation where we justify our failure to achieve something, by convincing ourselves that it was not worth achieving in the first place. No doubt mediators often wish the parties could adopt such an attitude in relation to the expected outcome. Those in conflict often hold the naïve view that 'winning' will render everything 'rosy' (see Chapter 8). A mediator can enable a party to question their conviction about the perceived benefits of a 'successful' outcome: to perhaps realize that there may be valuable outcomes other than merely winning; and that their entire world does not hinge upon a victorious conclusion.

We must not overlook the fact that the parties will also hold certain 'internal' perceptions of themselves. This will be in addition to their 'external' perception of the dispute and their view of the other persons involved in it. Our self-concept forms the basis of nearly all existentialist exploration. Kierkegaard sought to provide answers to the questions of who and what we are from a purely subjective standpoint: we must choose who or what we are, and live with the *anxiety* that this creates. Heidegger considered the phenomenon of authenticity: living authentically involves an in-depth understanding of ourselves, our responsibilities and possibilities. For Sartre, existence precedes essence, which means we start as nothing and move forward then to define ourselves through the exercise of the freedom to choose and by the choices we ultimately make. The common ground between these propositions is that we aim to live according to the values and value systems that we create for ourselves. When we fail to live up to these principles, when we fail to live in line with our values, our perception of ourselves contrasts with the perception as we would wish to see it. The result is that we disapprove of ourselves and our self-esteem is diminished.

The difficulty presented by this desire to live our lives authentically and according to our values is that we are likely to have one view of how we *ought* to live, and another of how we are *actually* living – and the two may cause an intra-psychic conflict. The 20th century mathematician and philosopher Bertrand Russell identifies this aspect of introspection as 'self-absorption', and in *The Conquest of Happiness* proposes that it is one of the principal causes of unhappiness. He takes three 'very common types' of personality: the sinner, the narcissist and the megalomaniac, and explains the causes of their unhappiness. First, the sinner:

When I speak of 'the sinner' I do not mean the man who commits sins: sins are committed by everyone and no one, according to our definition of the word; I mean the man who is absorbed in the consciousness of sin. This man is perpetually incurring his own disapproval, which if he is religious, he interprets as the disapproval of God. He has an image of himself as he thinks he ought to be, which is in continual conflict with his knowledge of himself as he is.

(1993: 6)

Similarly, the narcissist has created a value system that depends upon others admiring and loving him. But as the narcissist can never secure the love and admiration of *all*, he will remain unfulfilled and unhappy. The megalomaniac, too, has a value based upon being all-powerful; but 'since no man can be omnipotent, a life dominated wholly by the love of power can hardly fail sooner or later to meet with obstacles that cannot be overcome' (1993, 10). The megalomaniac is thus doomed to fail in his aspirations, and is condemned to constant unhappiness. The existentialist would say that the unhappiness of the sinner, the narcissist and the megalomaniac is caused by the failure to achieve the realization of their respective values, thereby causing them to experience intra-psychic conflict, and a loss of self-esteem.

Our self-perceptions are often idealistic and naïve, seeing ourselves as rational and sensible even when others see us as foolish and unreasonable. The perceptions of parties in dispute are similarly unrealistic, with the parties seeing themselves as 'the only normal reasonable persons in the dispute', while perceiving the others as 'abnormal' and perverse. In Chapter 2, this was compared to drivers who considered the slower drivers to be idiots and the faster ones to be maniacs, while at the same time seeing themselves as the only normal drivers on the road.

The Good Enough Principle

Such examples of a party's self-concept make it all the more problematic for the mediator to secure a perception shift. The shift in attitude, however, which has been repeatedly identified in previous chapters as a prerequisite to settlement, does not necessarily involve a *complete volte-face*. The mediator need secure only a small movement away from a party's view of the perfect idyllic resolution. The modification may be merely to a lesser position, namely one which, though not ideal, is nevertheless one with which 'they can live'. This is often termed the 'good enough' principle, whereby parties are urged to consider whether the resolution offered, though not ideal, is 'good enough' for them. It is derived from the writings of Donald W. Winnicott, a 20th century English paediatrician and psychoanalyst. He proposed the view that parents who strive constantly to be perfect parents may do themselves and their children more harm than if they were content to be 'good enough' parents. In litigation terms, the 'good enough' principle enables the parties to re-evaluate and reassess their aims and aspirations, so that they reach an objective point where they can state: 'This may not be as good as I had hoped for; but it is *good enough* for me.' The effective psychotherapeutically-trained mediator will aim to assist each party to analyse their options and possibilities, enabling them to establish what a realistic and appropriate level might be for a 'good enough' position.

8

Practical Application of Psychology in the Mediation Process

Previous chapters have sought to illustrate the nature and effect of the existential givens that are shared by all those in conflict. Parties in mediation similarly share a number of existential attributes: they all grapple with significant levels of uncertainty; they struggle against the elements of time and transiency; they are surrounded by ever-present emotions; they have a critical need to be heard; and they are constantly striving to maintain their self-esteem and cope with their values. These experiences translate into a broad variety of behavioural strategies that parties deploy during the mediation process, and which a mediator will be required to manage. These can cause problems for mediators if they are not handled effectively, and some of them will be examined more closely below.

Reluctance to Mediate

The first challenge for the mediator is to overcome the parties' fixated desire to litigate, and their psychological reluctance to mediate.

Parties in conflict want their 'day in court'. They prefer victory over compromise. It seems more 'natural' to resolve conflicts through battle – whether legally with armies of lawyers through the courts or militarily with armies of soldiers on the battlefield. Resolving conflicts through mediation is not an intuitive process. To sit down at the mediation table with their arch-enemy is asking much of the parties; to be expected additionally to compromise, to make concessions and to collaborate with that enemy is an anathema. Parties in conflict have a natural and powerful desire to be proved right and to 'win', so compromise does not come easily to them. It is often said that mediation has been a traditional method of conflict resolution 'since time immemorial' – when the 'wise man' or head of the village would act as mediator. This is not entirely accurate. The wise man more probably acted as judge or arbitrator, rather than a mediator; and the process would have been more akin to litigation than mediation, with each side presenting their case and inviting a decision to be made. The decision would thus be imposed upon them rather than reached by mutual and consensual agreement, and would be binding.

The attraction of litigation, therefore, is that it provides an almost unique opportunity for a person to be proved right – and to see the enemy punished. The desire to be proved right has long been regarded, from an intellectual standpoint, as a noble struggle for justice. In *The Republic*, Plato writes:

But what of the man who thinks he is wronged? Does he not then fume and chafe and fight on the side of what he believes to be just? Though he suffer hunger and cold, and every kind of privation, he perseveres till he conquers, and never desists from his noble indignation, until he has either accomplished his purpose or perished, or until reason within him calls him back as a shepherd calls his dog, and he relents.

(*Plato: The Republic 441*, trans. Lindsay, 1719)

This desire to litigate and to secure a decision in one person's favour at the expense of the other is problematic for the mediator. In order to be of assistance to the parties, the mediator needs fully to understand the precise psychological influence that this strong desire to triumph has over the mediation process. To win, a party has four essential needs that must be satisfied:

- the need for vindication – to be proved right
- the need for revenge – for the other party to feel the same or similar pain
- the need for humiliation – for the other party to be shamed
- the need for compensation – to recover perceived losses.

The mediator will need to differentiate between psychological 'needs' on the one hand and 'aspirations, desires and wishes' on the other. Needs, if they are truly 'necessities', are not capable of being negotiated. Aspirations, on the other hand, are susceptible to being adjusted and modified, whether through negotiation, logical persuasion, or otherwise. The four above-mentioned 'needs' can be examined in turn.

Vindication

The desire for vindication is a powerful driving force in litigation. Litigants hold a firm belief that they are right, and so being proved right provides an enormous boost to their self-esteem. This belief in the validity and justice of their cause may have been maintained over a lengthy period, and possibly endured in the face of strong opposing views from lawyers, experts, spouses and friends. Thus the need to be proved right becomes even stronger, propelling parties relentlessly towards the courts to seek that vindication. They hold on to the perhaps naïve view that the one person who will vindicate them is the judge. In the face of this need, it may not be appropriate or helpful for the mediator to explain that mediation is not about 'proving who is right and who is wrong'. The mediator may be more successful by persuading parties that at mediation they have the unique opportunity to demonstrate, face-to-face, across the table, and in a 'safe' environment, in the presence of all lawyers and others, that they are right and to prove to the other party that they are wrong.

Revenge

Revenge is a basic and primitive desire for retribution, and follows instinctively from a perceived injustice. For those who see themselves to be the victims of a grave wrong or unfairness, it may not even be sufficient to win; they will want to see blood on the walls. So revenge offers an opportunity to see others suffer similar pain to that which was inflicted. Such desire is timeless; it is noted in the second book of the Bible: 'An eye for an eye, a tooth for a tooth ...' (Exodus 21:24).

The knowledge that the perpetrator is suffering or will suffer the same or similar pain is curiously satisfying. Retribution can thus have a 'cathartic function' for those who have been affronted and angered by a transgression (Deutsch, Coleman and Marcus, 2006). A mediator will therefore require considerable empathic skills to enlighten parties that mediation is 'not necessarily about retribution'; but that nevertheless, seeing the other party 'squirm' from a verbal onslaught of reason and logic might be just as satisfying.

Humiliation

Humiliation is again a similar primordial desire: a need to debase and shame, creating a cathartic effect comparable to retribution. Mahatma Gandhi stated in *An Autobiography: The Story of My Experiments with Truth*, 'It has always been a mystery to me how men can feel themselves honored by the humiliation of their fellow beings' (Gandhi: 1993). The mystery is solved by understanding that humiliation of our enemies can provide us with a sense of power: it reinforces a perception of superiority over an inferior. But the mediator may wish to remind parties that Gandhi is also believed to have said 'an eye for an eye only ends up making the whole world blind'. The cathartic and therapeutic effect of the mediation process, whereby parties are able to feel heard, will often assuage the need for a sense of power and superiority, and so diminish the desire for humiliation.

Compensation

Compensation, and retribution, at their purest levels, may be born out of a commercial need to recoup losses. Yet the concept of 'recouping a loss' has a deeply emotional element. We are generally 'loss-averse': our fear of loss is often greater than the attraction of gain (Cialdini: 1984). It is therefore unfortunate that mediation has acquired a reputation for inevitably necessitating compromise. Hence litigants fear that they will be forced to make valuable concessions, and this plainly represents an element of loss, particularly when it is a loss of something to which they felt rightly entitled. We have seen (Chapter 3) how nearly all conflict is about loss: actual, potential, past, present or future loss. Our attitude towards loss will therefore be a powerful determining factor in our decision-making processes; it will govern our approach to and fear of *potential* loss, as well as informing our coping mechanisms for dealing with *actual* loss. In this way, litigation, together with other forms of 'retaliation', may be seen as a means of coping with loss.

The issue is made yet more complex by a realization that the mediator will have a similar aversion to loss and a corresponding desire to 'win'. A settlement may therefore represent a win, whereas if the parties are unable to settle, the mediator may consider himself to have suffered a loss. Clearly if this desire on the part of the mediator to achieve a settlement is allowed to gain dominance, it is likely to impede the progress to resolution. So mediators may need first to recognize and address these potentially destructive drivers of conflict *within themselves*, before seeking to assist parties to do so in mediation.

Problems in Pre-Mediation Contact

The Harvard model of 'shuttle' mediation, used in most commercial mediations in the UK, is said 'usually' to start with a joint session, with all parties around the table. There is, however, an increasing tendency to commence the mediation process with a series of separate private 'caucus' sessions as soon as the parties have arrived at the agreed venue. There is nevertheless still an important stage that *precedes* the arrival of the parties at the mediation venue: the pre-mediation contact between the parties and the mediator. Once appointed, the mediator will invariably contact the parties, whether by email, telephone, or in face-to-face meetings, to finalize details regarding the logistics of the mediation. These will include securing agreement as to the venue, the identity of the parties who will or will not attend, the length and duration of the mediation process, and, perhaps last but not least, the fee for the mediator. It is during these pre-mediation meetings that the mediator must begin the task of applying psychology in order to develop a trusting relationship, and to build rapport.

The pre-mediation stage is a period during which the emotions of the parties are likely to be heightened and raw. Parties are filled with anxiety about the uncertainties of the process; they perceive ulterior motives and express suspicion at each proposal made by the other party. This is where Husserl's method of phenomenology might come to the mediator's aid. Each party sees the other not as the persons that they are, but as the people they appear to them to be. In other words, Mr X is not merely the CEO of another company, he is Mr X, the 'person who is making false claims', or the 'person denying all fault'. Either way, Mr X represents 'the man who cannot be trusted'.

This distrust may first reveal itself in the process of selecting the mediator. The parties and their legal advisers will spend considerable time agonizing over the selection of the most appropriate mediator.

They invariably make their selection, not on the basis of which mediator might have the greatest and most relevant experience, but, rather, upon the basis of which mediator is more likely to vindicate them. Thus, for example, if a litigant has a claim against a bank, he or she will wish to select a mediator with some banking experience displayed in their CV; for this will be seen as the strongest likelihood of the mediator being 'on their side': 'If he knows anything about banking, he will immediately see that I am right.' The other party will be assumed to be making the choice of mediator on a similar basis. Hence the concern often expressed in such situations: 'If the mediator is good for them, then he must be bad for us.' The same will apply in the selection of a venue: any suggestion for an appropriate venue made by one party will be treated with suspicion by the other, as there will be an assumption that the proposed venue will in some way provide that party with an advantage. This pattern of suspicion-filled behaviour can permeate all pre-mediation negotiations, whether in relation to the date and timing of the mediation, the disclosure and exchange of documents or 'position statements', and in relation to the attendance or non-attendance of certain persons involved in the dispute. The psychologically informed mediator will recognize these displays as the product of anxiety caused by uncertainty. Their self-esteem is affected and generates undue fears of manipulation: each party is hypersensitive to the prospect of the other party exercising some controlling influence to secure an advantage. So emotions obscure judgment, and subjective interpretations lead to misperceptions and false assumptions. These constitute a multiplicity of coping mechanisms for preserving self-esteem, all being brought to the fore. The deployment of all the mediation skills in the mediator's repertoire begins here. By curbing his or her own impatience and frustration in the face of such childlike 'game-playing', the mediator can gain the trust of the parties. By listening without judgment or criticism, and through demonstrating empathy and understanding, the mediator can help parties overcome these early anxieties and fears; and this in turn may enable the mediator to begin building rapport. If successful, the parties begin to open up and unburden themselves of their doubts and uncertainties; they start to reveal details of their dispute, providing the mediator with high-context information, and, in turn, creating an opportunity to identify issues that may be important or sensitive in the dispute. This pre-mediation phase of the mediation process is both underused and its importance underestimated by many mediators. The communications that take place in these early and initial stages can prove vital in placing the dispute on the right path towards resolution.

Problems at the Mediation Venue

Being conscious of the heightened emotional state in which parties arrive at the mediation, the mediator will need to do everything possible to ensure that the venue provides a safe and comfortable environment for the process. 'Safe', as has already been indicated, does not necessarily refer to safety from a physical perspective, nor does 'comfort' signify only the corporal wellbeing of the parties. The mediator must try to eliminate all potential problems that may give rise to mental, emotional or psychological – as well as physical – discomfort. Some of these problems are considered below.

Rooms

By arriving early at the venue, the mediator can ensure not only that the rooms are suitably comfortable physically – that is, properly heated, ventilated, air-conditioned and lit; but also appropriately 'appointed'. That means, for example, that the rooms are adequately separated and sound-proofed, rather than divided by merely a thin plasterboard partition. If parties have even the slightest fear, however irrational, of their discussions being overheard, it will not be conducive to open and candid conversations. Similarly, if the rooms are situated in such a way that the parties have constantly to pass each other in the corridor whenever taking a break from proceedings, this may lead to an unduly apprehensive and uneasy atmosphere throughout the day. Again, mediators need to bracket any natural irritation they may feel at such foibles when they are raised and vocalized by the parties. Instead, the mediator is likely to benefit by showing empathy and understanding, and by being seen to address the concerns empathically.

The seating arrangements, both for joint sessions and private caucus sessions, will additionally require sensitive care and thought. Much has already been written about how optimally to arrange the seating (see, for example, Strasser and Randolph, 2004: 77), and it is not necessary to reiterate it here. Suffice it to say that the prudent mediator, when deciding upon which party is to occupy which room, or who should sit where at the table in the joint session, will have in mind the aspects of self-esteem, emotions, perceptions, and the parties' need for control, when addressing all these issues.

Joint Meetings

Joint sessions are meetings where parties are together around a table or in one room in order to exchange views or engage in a dialogue. They allow the parties to be introduced to each other, and so to be clear as to who is present and attending the mediation. Joint sessions in mediation are generally considered to be beneficial. They offer a number of opportunities and possibilities, which, even if not fully seized or fulfilled, can be valuable to the process. Nevertheless, however valuable the mediator believes such joint sessions to be, the parties should not be placed under any undue pressure to participate if they are hesitant or unwilling.

Benefits

Joint meetings offer a platform for a party to express their feelings, whether of anger, hurt, disappointment, betrayal – or joy. These joint meetings can create opportunities for a party to be listened to in a safe environment, and perhaps feel properly heard. At the same time they allow a party to listen directly to the other, rather than to have their views and sentiments transmitted through the words of another. This can often lead to both sides feeling more fully engaged in the process. A further important factor is that such joint meetings afford a unique prospect of dispelling misperceptions and correcting wrongful assumptions. As already discussed, parties will have built up perceptions of the parties on the other side of the conflict. These may have become rigid and sedimented views. The parties may never have met before, or alternatively a considerable amount of time may have elapsed since a previous meeting. Mental images will have been imprinted upon minds; and fixed notions implanted about the behaviours and motivations of others. The opportunity to see the other person in the flesh, and to hear their words spoken directly by them, can have a constructive effect. A common misperception often attaches to the competency or otherwise of the other side's lawyers. Each side's lawyers may have been demonized and dehumanized by the other, and their respective skills and expertise criticized and denigrated. By seeing these lawyers at the mediation in the joint meeting, the parties may be able to correct their perceptions, as they are able to see that these lawyers are human, capable and perhaps even reasonable. Even in situations where none of these perceptions are dispelled – and the opposite is more accurate so that the perceptions are reinforced – a clearer and more concrete understanding is achieved.

The benefits of the joint meeting will nearly always outweigh any disadvantages. So even where a party has not felt properly heard; or where they have not had a proper opportunity to express their views, or, indeed, where their previous views and assumptions have been confirmed, an element of uncertainty may nevertheless have been addressed or possibly eliminated. This can take the process constructively further down the route towards settlement than might be achieved by a series of separate and private meetings. Even where the exchanges between the parties have been heated and aggressive, it may at least be said that a dialogue has taken place.

In light of the benefits of joint meetings as described above, it may be helpful to consider, from a psychological viewpoint, some of the reasons and explanations that are offered for not agreeing to such joint discussions. The rationalizations for hesitation or refusal to participate in a joint meeting will differ from one person to another, and will vary from case to case. The legal advisers may have reasons quite dissimilar to those of the parties for refusing; and the mediator may possibly have his or her own justification for keeping the parties apart. In many instances, that justification will be linked to the existential concepts of uncertainty and control. All those involved in the conflict, as noted in previous chapters, will have a concern about the unpredictability of any stage in the process. A joint meeting will be seen as bringing with it a range of unforeseeable risks, all potentially adverse to a satisfactory settlement. The parties will be anxious as to where a joint meeting might lead if the emotions escalate excessively and the discussions spiral out of control. A mediator lacking in experience may be equally affected by such fear and anxiety. The lawyers will have added concerns: they may question the benefit of such a meeting when the parties are widely and diametrically apart; and they may be apprehensive as to how their clients will be judged in terms of their potential as good or bad witnesses. In the last of these circumstances, it may assist the mediator to point out the following: if the lawyer's client is likely to be a good witness then the sooner the other side are given the opportunity to make that judgment the better; and if the client is likely to be a poor witness, then, equally, the sooner the better that both the client and his or her own lawyer come to that realization.

In all these situations it will nevertheless be unhelpful and indeed counter-productive for the mediator to be seen as exerting pressure upon the parties or their lawyers to adopt a particular course of action in relation to a joint meeting – whether to participate or to refrain from so doing – if it is against the wishes of that party. In order to maintain a 'safe' environment, it is vital that the process remains consensual throughout, and that no person at the mediation is at any stage made to feel pressured or compelled to act against their better judgment. This may be difficult where the mediator is convinced one way or another as to whether a joint session will or will not be beneficial. In these circumstances, the mediator should bear in mind the need to bracket such beliefs, and the need to 'follow' rather than to 'lead'. Greater difficulties arise, of course, if one party or one member of 'the team' believes that a joint meeting should take place, and the other party, or another member of the team, is of the opposite view. In such instances, the mediator will need to do what he or she is there to do: mediate. He or she will explore with the persons on each side of the argument their respective fears and concerns, and so help them to analyse their way through the dilemma.

Preparing Parties for Joint Sessions

Joint meetings in a Harvard model of 'shuttle' mediation may take place at the very outset of the process, almost immediately after the parties have arrived at the venue. Alternatively, they may take place at a much later stage, after the parties have had a series of private caucus sessions. In many instances, they may not take place at all, with the parties remaining apart and in their separate rooms throughout the entire process. Where joint meetings do take place, they may involve a variety of permutations: all members of both party's 'team' might be present; or only part of the team; or the entire team on one side and part only of the team on the other; or just lawyers and experts; or just parties; or, indeed, any combination of the above. The preparation and lead-in time for these joint meetings will vary considerably. If the parties agree that a joint meeting is useful at the very start of the mediation, there may be very little opportunity for much 'preparation' of the parties by the mediator. The mediator may then simply outline the procedure to be adopted at the meeting; he or she may discuss with the parties who should or should not be present, and establish the order in which the parties will be expected to speak. (The issue as to who speaks first is dealt with in greater detail further below in this chapter.)

In preparing the parties for the joint session, the mediator may go on to consider with each party what they will or will not discuss. The mediator may guide the parties in relation to the purpose of the joint meeting and what they might expect to achieve by it. Mediators differ as to the extent of the 'coaching' that they should or should not provide to the parties. Some are 'expansive' in their guidance, encouraging the parties to say as much as possible, and in whatever manner they wish, about the issues that concern them in the conflict. Others may be more prescriptive and restrictive, advising parties what to say and how to say it – or what not to say. This author believes in informing the parties that the joint meeting is their *opportunity* to say whatever they feel they need or wish to say; that there is no restriction on what they should or should not say, nor, indeed, any real constraint upon the manner in which it is said. 'We are not in a church or a cathedral; nor are we in court where there are rules of evidence and rules of procedure.' This may be seen as contrary to the custom adopted by some mediators, who, as described previously (see Chapter 3), advise the parties to 'refrain from being confrontational'; to avoid saying anything 'too inflammatory'; and to sidestep any temptation to 'raise the temperature unduly'. Such an approach yet again stems from the mediator's fear of uncertainty, and a corresponding desire to be and to remain in control. Provocative confrontations that may result in excessive displays of emotion are dreaded, for they are signposts towards the possibility of an unpredictable outcome, wherein the mediator – as well as possibly others in the room – may feel they are losing control. Furthermore, as we noted in Chapter 3, the Anglo-Saxon temperament is uncomfortable with profuse displays of emotion: they seem to engender a high level of discomfort among many in conflict situations. It seems to be for this reason that mediators urge the parties to avoid creating such emotional conditions; and that when, despite their efforts, these emotional scenes occur they shy away from them by urging restraint or suggesting a short break from the proceedings. This is a regrettable approach. It wholly ignores the powerfully revelatory effect of emotional outbursts in a mediation setting.

As has also been illustrated in Chapter 3, emotions are the 'royal road' to the worldview of the party. They will reveal the party's values and value system, and the manner in which those values are being degraded. Anger will reveal where the injustice is perceived, where the hurt lies and what past loss has been suffered and what future loss is feared. The emotions may reveal precisely what it is that lies at the root of the conflict. It may be equally important for others in the mediation room, those beyond just the parties, also to observe where the emotions lie. Lawyers will often be wholly unaware of the reasons for the other party's stance; they may be baffled by their intransigence. The emotions they observe being displayed by the other party will provide them with a prime insight into the drivers that precipitate and prolong the dispute. Occasionally, it is the emotions displayed by their own clients that can be revelatory: clients often behave in a totally different manner in the presence of their lawyers than they do when confronted by an opposing party in mediation. Lawyers have been known to admit that they saw their client in a different light for the first time when they observed a heated exchange in the mediation joint meeting.

The mediator can therefore glean a great deal from the behaviour and emotional demeanour of the parties, and their entire entourage, when they confront each other around the table in a joint session. This does not mean that the mediator should *encourage* exhibitions of emotion, but merely that, when they occur, they should be seen as helpful gifts both to the mediator and possibly to the process as a whole. It promotes a better mutual understanding of 'where each party is coming from', and such understanding can accelerate the reconciliation process.

A slightly different approach to the coaching or preparation of parties may be required in certain instances where a joint meeting is proposed in order to achieve a certain and more specific objective. Examples for this can be found where a joint meeting is suggested so that one party may deliver an apology to the other; or where the lawyers suggest a meeting to explain their understanding of the relevant law; or when the experts agree to meet so as to clarify any disparate opinions. These cases will differ from the initial joint session, where parties meet in order simply to afford an opportunity for an initial and more general exchange of views. In later joint meetings, where a more specific agenda is proposed, there may be a greater efficacy in more extensive preparation of the parties by the mediator. The mediator is likely to be in an advantageous position: he or she will have explored and fully ascertained the perceived particular aims and objectives of each party in having a further joint meeting. Through similar probing investigations, the mediator will have acquired a good understanding of the nature and extent of the issues put forward by each party, together with a full appreciation of their expectations. For example, in relation to an apology, a skilful mediator will have secured a comprehensive picture of the reasons behind one party seeking an apology from the other: the mediator will have established the nature of the harm or injustice for which the apology is being demanded; and will have achieved an understanding of that party's expectations in relation to the terms of the apology. Thus the mediator can gain clear insights into the type of apology that will or will *not* be acceptable. Turning to the offeror, the mediator will have examined the nature and substance of the proposals for the apology, and will be aware of the specific content proposed, as well as the outcome that the offeror anticipates to secure by making the apology. Armed with this comprehensive knowledge of the aims of one party and the expectations of the other, the mediator is in a good position to guide each party appropriately, and to ensure as far as possible that the expectations and the aims of the two parties correspond and coincide. This will avoid the all too common situation whereby one party offers an apology that is deemed wholly inadequate, or which fails properly to address the relevant issues, or is in relation to an issue which was not that anticipated by the other. Such misapprehensions simply result in an escalation of the disappointment, frustration and anger.

Setting Ground Rules

If, as is suggested here, an element of emotional behaviour is to be tolerated in joint sessions, some boundaries may need to be set. Behaviour that causes discomfort might be helpful in some instances, but can also be counter-productive in others. In setting boundaries, the mediator will need to assess each situation in its context and on its own merits, dependent upon the identity of the parties and the nature of the dispute. Parties are frequently more at ease with presentations of anger or distress than other 'non-parties' in the room, whether they are the legal advisers, friends, or even the mediator. But all will need to be made properly aware of the mediator's approach in such situations. It is not helpful if those in the room question why the mediator is permitting such behaviour to continue, when they would prefer it to be halted. Thus, if the mediator is one who believes that a certain level of emotion – be it anger, rage, or grief – is both inevitable and possibly constructive, the parties will need to be clearly informed about the boundaries. The mediator should have a good understanding of the degree of emotional behaviour that is likely to be tolerated by the parties in the room before it becomes destructive; and will therefore need to make clear the extent to which such behaviour will be permitted. All parties should be given some indication as to when and how the mediator proposes to intervene; and an indication of the aspects of conduct and verbal expression that are and are not likely to be acceptable. In this way, all those in the room at a joint meeting will be reassured that the process is well under the control of the mediator, and will be less prone to unease and anxiety when behaviour is seen as approaching – or overreaching – the boundaries of acceptability.

Who Speaks First?

Once the joint meeting has commenced, and the mediator has given a short introductory opening statement, the parties will be invited to make their opening statements. The order in which parties are asked to speak in the joint meeting, as with seating and other arrangements, is an important issue requiring some thought on the part of the mediator. The selection process as to who is invited to make their statement first can present the mediator with a dilemma. It is likely that undue weight will be attributed by the parties to the mediator's choice, and it may well be viewed as overly meaningful by them. With emotions very much on the surface, and the parties being hypersensitive to any possible partiality by the mediator, there is a danger that parties will infer greater significance in the selection of the first speaker than may be intended by the mediator: 'Why is the other side being asked to put their case first and before ours?' The mediator, if sensitive to this, will be conscious of the need for each party to be 'in control' and for their self-esteem to be protected. The mediator should therefore consider with care the appropriate explanation for the selection. It will need to be wholly divorced from the facts of the case, so as to avoid any possible inference that some form of judgment has been made as to the respective merits of each party's case. A possible neutral rationalization for choosing one party to make their opening statement first or to speak before the other is to identify the claimant or the person bringing the claim or complaint. 'It is traditional in the English legal system for the claimant to "go first"': such an explanation may suffice to placate those who might have concerns of bias.

Enforcing Ground Rules

The setting of ground rules can create safety in providing boundaries for behaviour, but it brings with it a corresponding obligation to enforce such rules and to see that they are respected by both sides. All boundaries and rules are capable of being renegotiated and reconsidered, and mediators are constantly reminded of the need to be flexible. Situations and circumstances change, people alter their positions, perspectives are transformed, and so commitments and promises, as in all aspects of life, may need re-evaluation. Nevertheless, the enforcement of such rules can be problematic for a mediator. This is especially so where it is important to build a friendly and trusting relationship with both parties, while striving to be seen throughout as entirely neutral. The more ground rules that are set, the more frequent are the occasions when the mediator will be called upon to enforce them. This can place the mediator overly in the role of a police officer or schoolmaster: someone who is perceived as 'putting parties in their place' when they have disobeyed. This can be especially challenging, since ground rules are invariably broken by one party in the presence of the other. It obliges the mediator to implement the 'ruling' while one party watches on – something that is likely to be seen as a benefit to one party, secured at the expense of the other.

A particular ground rule that provides a good example of this, and frequently causes problems for a mediator, is in relation to 'interruptions'. It is the practice of some mediators to urge each party to refrain from interrupting the other in the joint session or during the opening statements. Some go further and insist upon a total absence of interruptions: 'Please allow the other person to speak and do not interrupt.' This author believes that such an approach is not helpful. It is often wholly unrealistic to expect even the most restrained of parties to maintain total silence while the other is speaking. They may hear accounts with which they will violently disagree; the assertions may be upsetting and offensive; or they may be considered misleading, inaccurate, false or untrue. The party listening will have a natural but forceful inclination to contradict, correct, or refute what is being said: they will not wish the assertions to pass without comment. The temptation in such circumstances to interrupt may be too great. If the mediator has set a ground rule prohibiting interruptions, he or she is then placed in the uncomfortable position of having to enforce that rule. It is uncomfortable because it may oblige the mediator to raise a hand in a 'stop!' gesture – and 'stop' gestures ought to have little part in the mediator's tool box. Such reprimands and other incitements to the party to 'obey the rules' can only adversely affect the development of a good relationship between mediator and party. Nor will they enhance the mediator's role as an unbiased neutral. The aggravating feature is that such admonishments, as has been noted above, will necessarily take place in the presence of the other party and will inevitably be interpreted in different ways. The party on the receiving end may sense embarrassment or humiliation, with a perception that they have been 'put down' by the mediator in the face of the other party. This inevitably leads to an interpretation that the mediator is biased against them. It may be equally inescapable that the other party will also interpret the mediator's actions as revealing that the mediator is 'on their side'.

It is important, therefore, that the mediator appreciates that the parties may make such analyses of these interventions even though they are made for the purpose of enforcing or implementing a ground rule or boundary. In such cases, where the mediator reasonably anticipates the joint opening session to be fraught with interruptions, it may be prudent to acknowledge this possibility at the outset. The mediator may need to emphasize, in an empathic manner, that interruptions, and indeed any emotional 'eruptions', are natural and to some extent inevitable; that being so, they will not be adversely judged or criticized when they occur. This then provides greater latitude to the mediator in deciding whether or not to intervene; and it is likely to reduce the number of occasions when intervention becomes necessary.

But however meticulously the mediator tries to prepare the parties for such incidents, they may nevertheless occur, and there will be occasions when the mediator feels duty-bound to intervene because the behaviour has become unduly destructive. Following these incidents, the mediator will need to redouble his or her efforts in repairing possible perceptions of lost neutrality. Some trust may have been diminished, and it will require rebuilding. The mediator can achieve this by demonstrating a compassionate understanding of the underlying emotions that precipitated the behaviour. Compassion in such circumstances need not necessarily involve partiality; and so, if expressed sensitively, can avoid an impression of one-sidedness, while overcoming a perception of bias in the opposite direction.

Walk-outs

Similar factors of empathy and compassion will apply when parties 'stage' a walk-out. A walk-out may be described as 'staged', where such conduct is an attempt to regain control of a 'losing' situation. Often this is a coping mechanism for loss of self-esteem: it provides a useful exit from a losing position, and avoids the ignominy of having to remain in that situation longer than necessary. It may also be perceived to be the most effective means of rendering the opponent entirely powerless: for they have no one left against whom to fight. The suggested ways of dealing with such incidents have previously been addressed by Strasser and Randolph (2004: 161). Nevertheless, it may be repeated here that it is vital for the mediator to show no judgment or criticism of this behaviour – even if and when convinced that it is staged. For though it appears to have been staged, it is likely to be a result of some loss of self-esteem on the part of the person walking out. This will only be intensified if they are made to feel further humbled or demeaned. It is important, therefore, for the party walking out to be 'managed' and spoken to *by the mediator*, rather than by any other person present. It may well be that the party effecting a walk-out is accompanied at the mediation by a lawyer or a friend. When such a walk-out takes place, the lawyer or friend may almost certainly volunteer to assist, by going out after the disappearing party in order to 'deal with the situation': 'Leave it to me: I'll go and speak to him.' This could prove unhelpful or even counter-productive. The lawyer or friend may not have had the benefit of mediation training, and so may not be psychotherapeutically informed. Consequently they may not be sufficiently skilled in absorbing the anger or in empathizing with the distress of the party walking out. They may not be aware of the appropriate way to respond to such a situation, and can easily aggravate rather than ameliorate the position. For example, they may suggest simply coming back into the room: this would amount to a complete lack of understanding as to the emotional causes of the walk-out, and would be an underestimation of the psychological effect of having to return to face the other party. Alternatively, the friend or lawyer may seek to support their friend or client, and encourage them to leave or remain out of the mediation process. Either way, it is unlikely to be helpful to the process. If the mediator fails to follow the party to speak to them outside, he or she will have no influence over what is said by the lawyer or friend, nor will there be any understanding of what has transpired while they are all outside. By leaving it to someone else to speak to or 'deal with' the party, the mediator will have relinquished an element of control of the process. An optimum suggested approach would be to welcome the assistance of the lawyer or friend, and to invite or allow them to accompany the mediator while the mediator speaks to the party outside. In this way, the mediator achieves several objectives: he or she engages with the lawyer or friend in a way that enhances their self-esteem, while retaining control over the handling of the party who has walked out.

Taking Notes

Strasser and Randolph (2004: 81) identify some of the problems created by the mediator taking notes when listening to the parties. It can plainly be a distraction for the parties continually to have an eye upon the mediator's pen. When they try to detect what the mediator is writing, they are not concentrating fully upon the account they are giving. When they are speculating as to the reasons for the mediator noting one thing while failing or refusing to note another, their minds are not wholly focused upon the narrative. The parties become overly conscious of what to say and what the mediator may expect them to say. They may also feel they are not being properly heard. This is more acute when the note-taking occurs in a joint session. Here, the parties will be doubly apprehensive, for not only are they concerned about what the mediator is writing, but they will also be conscious of the interpretations likely to be put upon the note-taking by the other party. Self-esteem again comes into play: 'What do the other party make of the mediator taking a note of what I am saying?' 'What was so important about what I just said? Might the other side assume that I said something damaging to me or useful to them?' 'Will this note be used against me – whether by the mediator, or, worse still, by the other party?'

It is suggested, therefore, that it is generally wise to avoid note-taking during the joint session. It creates undue opportunities for a perception of bias. These perceptions of bias are not born of rational or logical thought, but, rather, will be the product of assumptions and 'subjective truths'. Furthermore, the mediator is unlikely even to be aware of these perceptions during the joint meeting. He or she is not in a position there and then to explore the understandings of the parties, and so cannot dispel any misconceptions that may have arisen. In a private session with individual parties, the mediator may be sensitive to any anxieties on the part of the speaker if and when notes are being taken, and so can more readily explore and examine any interpretations being made. Nevertheless, this author would urge caution when making notes even in private session. There will, of course, be some occasions when it may not only be advisable but necessary to take notes, and these are discussed below; however, in most other circumstances the note-taking can be carried out either in the 'shuttle periods' between private sessions, or possibly by a co-mediator or assistant. In any event, it should wherever possible be carried out openly and expressly, with all concerned being made aware of what is being written and why.

Having argued generally against note-taking, it is nevertheless necessary to acknowledge, as indicated above, that there are many occasions when it will not only be wise to do so, but of crucial importance. Many disputes will involve a plethora of complex facts and figures. It is a contention of this book that the real dispute will commonly lie, not in the facts and figures, but in the psychological make-up of the people involved: see Nietzsche's proposition: 'There are no facts, only interpretations'. Nevertheless, there will be many disputes where the mediator will need to have a reasonable grasp of the underlying factual or mathematical data that underpin the conflict. In these circumstances the failure to take notes may in fact create a level of mistrust and doubt in the minds of the parties as to the capabilities of the mediator. On these occasions, the prudent mediator will indicate to the parties what is being noted and why it is being noted. It is again suggested that, to avoid a perception of bias, this should rarely occur in joint meetings, and should better be reserved for the private caucus sessions. Any complex matters raised in the joint meetings can always be further explored and explained in private.

A further instance in which it may be vital for the mediator to take notes is when messages, offers and proposals are expressly given to the mediator by one party to be taken across to the other. If the message is short and plain, there may be little expectation that it will be written down. However, where the matters to be passed on to the other party are more complex or numerous, it may be helpful both to the mediator and to the parties if appropriate notes are taken. Examples of such instances are where:

- there are complicated or numerous issues
- there are both positive and negative messages
- only certain matters are to be transmitted while others are to remain confidential
- the matters involve sensitive information and require complete accuracy in transmission.

In all these cases, the taking of notes creates reassurance for all concerned, and thus contributes to a 'safer' process. The notes can then be read over to the party and checked before the message is transmitted to the other side. It has a threefold benefit:

- the notes will ensure that the mediator has an accurate formulation of the message that is to be transmitted

- the notes, when read back, will enable the party to correct any errors or inaccuracies, and so will reassure them that the precisely intended message is being taken across

- the notes will reassure the mediator, when passing the message on, that he or she has accurately and comprehensively noted and delivered the appropriate message.

A practical analogy of this can be seen in the following vignette: a hotel guest telephones Reception to request an early morning wake-up call. The guest gives his or her name, the room number and the time requested for the alarm call. The hotel receptionist takes the call but makes no reference to the details nor does he or she repeat them back to the guest. The guest is then left anxious as to whether the message was noted down accurately – or at all; or whether there is likely to be any confusion as to the name, or the room number, or the time. If, on the other hand, the receptionist expressly makes a note, and reads back to the guest the details noted, the guest will be reassured that the correct name and room number have been recorded – and can sleep comfortably in the expectation of being woken at the correct time. Parties in mediation will have similar anxieties. When the mediator leaves the room and walks along the corridor to deliver the message to the parties in the other room, they will have parallel fears. 'Has the mediator accurately memorized the message?' 'Will the message be delivered correctly?' 'Might the mediator mistakenly impart confidential information that they had revealed in the private session and which they had asked to remain undisclosed?' 'Or is there a danger that the mediator might inadvertently confuse the information given?' Such uncertainties are unhelpful in maintaining the trusting relationship; hence note-taking in these instances can serve to avoid these anxieties.

In some cultures across the globe, note-taking is viewed as a prerequisite to being taken seriously. In the more bureaucratic societies the absence of note-taking is likely to detract from the credibility and authority of the mediator, and therefore impinge upon the creation of trust. In these circumstances, the mediator may need to consider and adapt the foregoing approach to note-taking. The mediator may need to develop alternative ways of taking notes that do not arouse a suspicion of bias, and do not give rise to possibilities of misinterpretations as to their significance. For example, the mediator may possibly devise a formula of explanatory words to clarify the purpose of the note-taking, or alternatively to persuade a party that the absence of note-taking should not be interpreted as a lack of serious interest.

The Settlement Agreement

The final stage of most mediations is the preparation and drafting of a settlement agreement. It is generally accepted that in commercial and other similar mediations, unless and until an agreement is put in writing and signed by both parties, any accord made will not be binding or enforceable upon either party. Consequently it is of considerable importance that the written settlement agreement is a good and valid record of all the settlement terms agreed between the parties. It therefore needs to be comprehensive, clear and wholly unambiguous. It is respectfully suggested that the mediator should retain a supervisory role in the preparation of all settlement agreements, irrespective of whether there are lawyers present and involved in the drafting. The courts abhor satellite litigation involving investigations into the terms and intentions of the parties, arising out of poorly drafted settlement agreements. It is thus the mediator's duty, as far as reasonably possible, to ensure that the agreement is unlikely to unravel, and that it includes all matters upon which agreement was reached. This may, for example, involve considering the inclusion of a clause dealing with the legal costs incurred by the parties leading up to the mediation – a matter all too often omitted or overlooked by even experienced mediators. It may also require a consideration of any practical issues left to be implemented, such as times for compliance, the terms of a written apology, or a reference, or some other written notice to be completed after the conclusion of the mediation. If matters are left to the parties to implement at a later stage, it is vital that the settlement agreement is precise and clear about every aspect of these obligations. It is all too easy, for example, to leave an apology or a reference to be drafted or written at a later time, after the conclusion of the mediation meeting. The danger of so doing is that the mediator no longer has control over what is written; and if the document that is eventually drafted transpires to be 'wholly unacceptable', the entire settlement may unravel.

The psychological difficulty for the mediator is that these agreements are invariably drafted at the end of a long day or following several lengthy sessions, when parties may be suffering from fatigue, hunger, frustration, disappointment, anger or irritability. Alternatively, the parties may be euphoric, and all too eager to part company on good terms, without paying sufficient close attention to the detailed terms of any settlement agreement. In either case, it is at this final stage of the mediation that the mediator will require copious amounts of patience and perseverance in the deployment of the psychological tenets set out in this book.

Self-esteem will once again play a fundamental role in the final deliberations over the detail of the agreement. Parties may feel bruised and battered from the effect of having had to 'compromise their positions unduly'; their values and value systems will have been tested and stretched to their limit; and they may still harbour some reservation as to whether or not they have been properly heard. They may still be struggling with uncertainty: lingering doubts remaining as to the wisdom of the choices they have made, and apprehension persisting in relation to the possible consequences of their actions. Their self-esteem will require protection and the mediator will need to be responsive to this.

Lawyers might be a separate or particular problem. They will have been present throughout the entire period of the mediation. They will have contributed to the process in various degrees: some will have been at the forefront of all negotiations, helping to analyse all steps and moves, and prominently helping in the formulation of offers and proposals for settlement. Others may have taken a much lesser role, allowing their clients to take the lead. In whichever way they have contributed to the process, the lawyers are likely to regard settlement agreements as matters that fall within their particular province and expertise; this may be where they seek to flex their muscles, and to demonstrate the usefulness and value of their presence – and thereby justify their fee. This can translate into what may appear to the mediator, and to the remaining parties, to be obstructive behaviour, with over-emphasis on legal niceties and technical details. This is a critical stage of the process, and the mediator can hasten the drafting process by being attentive to the needs and self-esteem of the lawyers, and by addressing their need also to be heard and valued at that stage of the proceedings.

9

Psychology in Differing Models of Mediation

Mediation is a relatively simple concept. The process involves little more than a neutral third party entering the dispute as a facilitator and assisting parties to resolve their conflict. The process is intended to be informal, without strict rules of procedure or rules of evidence. The same model can be used by the rich and by the poor, in large claims as well as those classified as Small Claims. It can be helpful in mulit-million-pound international commercial disputes; and can also be invoked by neighbours in minor community disputes. The same concept of a neutral facilitator will resolve conflicts between employees in the workplace; between family members and spouses in the home; and can be used between victim and perpetrator in the criminal justice system. The process should therefore be freely transferable between all forms of dispute in every sector.

Yet the mediation world has regrettably formed itself into silos, with relatively distinct and differing models of mediation being used in civil/commercial cases, in family and divorce cases, in employment and workplace conflicts, in community and neighbour clashes, and in restorative justice procedures. The practitioners in each model of mediation passionately believe that their approach is to be preferred and their evangelism has possibly caused the silo effect. For example, many commercial mediators find it difficult to comprehend how family mediators can conduct entire mediations without going into private caucus (see further below): they find it difficult to appreciate how conflicts can effectively be resolved without parties having an opportunity to mention matters to the mediator in private and in confidence, and which they would not wish to say openly to the other party. Conversely, family mediation practitioners are equally adamant that their conflicts need to be resolved openly, collaboratively and 'without secrets'. It may be similarly incomprehensible to them that workplace and neighbour disputes are frequently resolved without the parties coming together at all during the mediation.

This is not the place to consider each model of mediation in any detail. Nor should it be necessary from a psychological viewpoint, having regard for the fact that all involve people, and so all share similar existential features. Whether dealing with business leaders, spouses, neighbours, employees or victims and criminal offenders, the mediator will encounter similar shared existential givens in each. Nevertheless, it is proposed to give a brief outline of the five models mentioned above, and to identify some of the psychological elements that may apply peculiarly to each.

Civil Commercial Mediation

The model of mediation adopted in the UK for civil commercial disputes – and the one principally espoused on the Mediation

Skills course at Regent's University London – is sometimes known as the Harvard model of 'shuttle' mediation. Some of the psychological features have been detailed in the previous chapter: it usually involves an initial joint session, where all parties meet around a table, followed by an indeterminate number of private caucus sessions, during which the mediator shuttles between the parties who are in separate rooms. Civil commercial mediation of disputes invariably take place in one venue and over a period of one or a few more days. The parties are usually encouraged to ensure that all decision-makers do attend and that they are able actively to participate. They are often invited to confirm that they have 'full authority to settle' the dispute, or, alternatively, if their authority is restricted, they may be required to indicate the limits of that authority. The aim of these stipulations is to ensure that, as far as possible, the mediation day is used to its fullest advantage, and that all aspects are conducive to resolving the conflict 'fully and finally'. If the ultimate decision-maker is absent, the process can be rendered ineffectual. Even when the decision-maker is 'on the end of a phone', it may still frustrate the success of a potential settlement. Thus it is important that all those involved in the dispute are able to witness the workings of the process at first hand. They need to experience the emotional roller-coaster that is produced when parties state their positions and express their sentiments, whether face-to-face or through the mediator. They benefit hugely from being able to observe and to sense for themselves the meaningful and often dramatic reactions when offers are made and rejected; when counter-proposals are received and analysed. Without being directly involved in the 'movements' that take place within a mediation, the decision-maker who is 'on the end of a phone', or otherwise absent, will have a distorted view of what has transpired, and so cannot provide a constructive and balanced opinion of any proposed settlement. The hearts of most mediators sink when they are told by the party: 'Let me just phone my spouse'; or 'Give me a moment while I call my lawyer'; or 'Let me check with my superiors'. When parties outside the mediation are asked to intervene, it often leads to unhelpful reactions on their part: they may find the settlement proposals 'outrageous', or 'utterly unacceptable', or 'a roll-over'. They will be of little assistance to those seeking seriously to negotiate a mutually acceptable solution.

The fact that commercial disputes are never devoid of emotion has already been considered (Chapter 3). It matters not how 'dry' or technical the issues may be, the dispute will always involve people, and so emotions are inescapable. The overpowering effect of emotions upon rational and commercial thought has been examined. Nevertheless, there is a factor in business-related disputes that can temper the influence of emotions, and that is the commercial imperative to resolve the conflict quickly and cheaply. It is extremely rare for it to be advantageous to a commercial organization to be in dispute with another. Even when the delaying factor of litigation might be beneficial in relation to timing or cash-flow issues, it is nearly always preferable, and likely to be more economic, to secure such delays by agreement rather than forcefully in litigation. Similarly, in intellectual property cases, the visibility of litigation may be important in order to deter others: where a party may wish the world to know that they will zealously protect their interest through the courts, it may nevertheless be preferable mutually to agree a formula for disseminating such awareness, without the need for costly and protracted lawsuits.

Reality Checks in Commercial Conflicts

In commercial disputes, the mediator always has this commercial card to play. By invoking the 'what if' question, the parties can be urged to analyse the positive commercial effects of settling and contrast these with the financial detriments of protracted litigation. The 'what if' principle involves both the miraculous and the catastrophic 'what if?' It is a challenge to the party, inviting them to reassess and re-evaluate their expectations, as well as their aims and aspirations, in the light of possible miraculous or catastrophic consequences. For example: 'What effect would it have upon your organization – and your family – if this matter were settled today and your company could draw a line underneath this episode, and concentrate on productivity and profit-making?' Or alternatively: 'How would it affect your company's reputation if this matter were to go to court and your conduct were to be heavily and publicly criticized?' By confronting the party with a best or worst-case scenario the mediator provides an opportunity, within the mediation process and together with the mediator, to contemplate and analyse the best and the worst that could happen. This will usually achieve one of two results:

- the party is able to shift their perception and re-evaluate their outlook upon the situation, by realizing that the worst scenario 'might possibly not be so bad after all' and that they could 'learn to live with it', or that what is being offered may in fact be 'good enough'

or

- the party realizes that such a situation is 'too awful even to contemplate', thereby facilitating an upward or downward shift from the originally held 'bottom-line' position.

In either case, the mediator is adopting and implementing the existentialist approach to the concept of 'freedom of choice', whether as advocated by Kierkegaard, Merleau-Ponty, or Sartre (see Chapter 1). Each party has the freedom to choose the path they wish to follow, and each choice has its possibilities as well as responsibilities. The mediator will nevertheless be conscious of the party's existential fear of uncertainty, their struggle with temporality and transiency and their desire to choose in accordance with their value systems.

It is for this reason that the catastrophic 'what if' question may be too confrontational a challenge if deployed at too early a stage in the mediation. The mediator needs to ensure that a sufficient level of trust and rapport has been achieved. Without this, the likelihood is that the mediator will risk the disaffection of the party on the receiving end. However, if used when parties have adopted rigid stances, and as a result may have become deadlocked, it can be an invaluable means of securing a shift in attitude.

A further and effective reality test in commercial disputes is to explore with the deadlocked party the cost of winning in court. It may be that the parties wish to exercise their freedom of choice by choosing the path to litigation, and that they are at an impasse because one or other feels that 'they will be better off going to court'. In these circumstances, it can be productive to analyse with the party in some detail the cost of winning in court. As previously stated, parties often have an overly positive perception of winning: 'all will be rosy if only the case can be won'. So by inviting the party to consider the high economic as well as the excessive social cost that will be involved in securing a successful outcome in court, the mediator may be in a position to soften a rigid stance. The party is thus urged to assess the cost not only in relation to irrecoverable legal expenses, but more in terms of time, energy, morale, family harmony, health and well-being,

Family Mediation

The mediation profession as a whole remains largely unregulated. There is little or no statutory or legislative control over the quality, training, or expertise of mediators; nor of the processes or procedures that must be adopted. Family mediators, however, are subject to a number of restrictions and controls:

- the Family Procedure Rules (FPR) and Practice Directions: these are Ministry of Justice Rules and Guidelines setting out procedures, standards and recommendations that are to be followed if parties wish to take their family or divorce dispute through the courts

- the Family Mediation Council (FMC) Code of Practice: this is a code of practice that 'applies to all family mediation conducted or offered by mediators who are members of the Member Organisations of the Family Mediation Council' (Para 1.1 FMC Code of Practice 2010). It governs the qualifications and training of mediators; the conduct of the mediation process, as well as certain ethical and legal principles to be followed by all mediators in family cases

The FMC Code of Practice extends deeply into the approach that mediators are expected to adopt in certain mediation situations. For example, when dealing with the Impartiality of the mediator (Para 5.1 and 5.4), the Code stipulates that:

Mediators must seek to prevent manipulative, threatening or intimidating behaviour by any participant. They must conduct the process in such a way as to redress, as far as possible, any imbalance of power between the participants. If such behaviour or any other imbalance seems likely to render the mediation unfair or ineffective, mediators must take appropriate steps to seek to prevent this including terminating the mediation if necessary.

(FMC Code Para. 5.4.2)

Again, when covering Abuse and Power Imbalances within the Family (Para 5.8), the Code prescribes the following conduct for the mediator:

Mediators must be alert to the likelihood of power imbalances existing between the participants.

(FMC Code Para 5.8.7)

and

> Mediators must seek to prevent manipulative, threatening
> or intimidating behaviour by either participant during the
> mediation.

(FMC Code Para 5.8.10)

This may be seen as cutting across the existentialist methodology, which would advocate *working with* and seeking to understand such behaviour, rather than trying to prevent or eliminate it (see further below).

Procedure in Family Mediation

The procedure for family mediation, as envisaged by the Family Procedure Rules, involves an initial meeting with both parties, usually separately (although they can be held with both parties present), followed by a series of sessions over a period of weeks, with both parties together. The initial meeting is known as a 'MIAM': a Mediation Information and Assessment Meeting, and is designed as an 'intake' meeting to enable a mediator to consider, with each or both of the parties together, whether or not mediation is suitable. Mediation will be deemed unsuitable if there are allegations of domestic violence or abuse or there appears to be a need for protection of either party (Practice Direction 3A, FPR 2010 SI No. 2955). This author would respectfully suggest that such restrictions can create an unfortunate missed opportunity – a chance to address these damaging and critical behaviours in a neutral and non-adversarial environment.

The MIAM is followed by a series of joint meetings with both parties together, but usually without legal advisers. These meetings are conducted over a period of weeks, with a maximum of six sessions, each lasting 90 minutes. The intervals between each session are designed to enable both parties to seek legal advice and to allow time for reflection. This clearly differs dramatically from the commercial model described above, where parties are actively discouraged from seeking the opinions of those who have not been present at the mediation session. Kate Aubrey-Johnson and Helen Curtis explain the advantages of periodic sessions with adequate intervals in this way:

> Where couples are dealing with the emotional trauma of a relationship breakdown, it is particularly important to have time to consider long-term decisions and to provide pause for thought at a time when they are stressed and emotionally vulnerable. Interim arrangements can be put in place during the intervening period. Being able to make temporary interim agreements has the advantage of being able to assess the implications over a period of time. Mediation should not urge couples to make decisions without thinking through the emotional and practical consequences.
>
> (2012: 266)

The psychological effect upon the mediator of this aspect of the family mediation model is significant. The mediator will need to anticipate changes in the parties and their issues at each session. All assumptions and perceptions made in relation to the specific matters agreed to or dealt with on previous sessions must be bracketed. The mediator will not be able to assume that the parties are in the same or similar position as when the previous session ended. Although this is true of all forms of shuttle mediation, it is more acute in the family model. When mediators leave one room in a commercial mediation in order to see the other party, they may well anticipate encountering a shift in position on their return, and while on occasions it may be as dramatic as a complete *volte-face*, it is more likely to be relatively minor. Each time couples return to a further family mediation session, they will have reflected at length upon their situation, and additionally will have been subjected to inputs from their lawyers, their relatives and families, and their friends and work colleagues.

Summarizing in family mediation joint sessions

A further variation in procedure from the civil commercial model is that the mediator at the joint session is expected to summarize each party's position in relation to their issues, demands and proposals, and this summary thus takes place in the presence of both parties. Students on the Regent's University London Mediation Skills courses are advised of the dangers of making any summary of one party's position in the presence of the other. The rationale for this is that it is likely to be impossible for the mediator to summarize one party's position in such a way as to avoid all or any perceptions of bias. The parties will crave the support and favour of the mediator. The choice of words used in the summary, the tone of voice, the perceived emphasis on some issues as opposed to others, the inclusion or omission of certain facts or topics – all these will be scrutinized by each person present; they will be analysed for their implications, and interpretations will be made as to what is in the mind of the mediator, and on which 'side' he or she stands. Even a wholly innocent question such as 'Is there anything else you would like to say at this stage?' may be capable of being analysed and misinterpreted. For example, it might be taken as an indication that the mediator knows more than the party is willing to say, or is in some way looking for further disclosure from that party. These are the perils of making statements about one party's case in front of the other. Marion Roberts, however, justifies it in this way:

> The advantages of this are threefold:
>
> - the parties are more likely to listen calmly to the mediator than to each other
>
> - the mediator is able to report the substance of the dispute and the accompanying strength of feeling (*that* the party feels strongly, *how* strongly they feel, and *what they feel strongly about*), but free of the angry tone, aggravating facial expressions and acrimonious language that could trigger off emotional recriminations and escalate the conflict
>
> - misunderstandings can be sorted out as early as possible.
>
> (1997: 111)

Justice and Power Imbalances

As long as the concept of fault remains a decisive element in divorce, perceptions of justice and injustice will abound. However, the justice as dispensed by the courts and 'higher authority' may appear wholly dissimilar to that felt by the parties. The concept of justice involves a form of moral objectivity, which, as Kierkegaard sought to show, is simply an illusion that cannot exist. Justice must remain subjective, a perception formed from each party's personal standpoint in a dispute. Mediators who shuttle from one party to another will experience mutual and overlapping perceptions of justice, which are likely to be wholly contradictory. Consequently, it is not the mediator's role or task to ensure that 'justice is done' between the parties. Nor should the mediator be seduced into applying his or her own understanding of the justice of the situation, for it is unlikely to be equally valid for both parties. The mediator should also bear prominently in mind that he or she may never have a comprehensive understanding of all the relevant facts. Take the position of a spouse who is about to accept a payment of £50,000 in settlement of one element of the dispute, whereas the mediator believes that a figure in the region of £500,000 might be more 'just'. The mediator might not be aware, for example, that the party is under extreme pressure from the bank to pay in funds to its account, in the absence of which the bank would foreclose upon the business and the home, and withdraw all lending facilities. In such circumstances, a settlement of £50,000 would be extremely attractive and, unbeknown to the mediator, might adequately serve the needs of the party notwithstanding that it appeared wholly 'unfair'.

Nevertheless, it is the view of many mediators that there is a duty to ensure that there are no undue imbalances of power in the process. Where such an imbalance gives the impression of one party having the ability to *influence* the mediator so as to secure a more favourable outcome, the mediator may need to be more circumspect. In such a situation, the mediator will need to redouble his or her efforts to demonstrate impartiality.

There is little doubt that where the mediator suspects or notes any element of duress, it may be necessary to intervene, or even to terminate the process. However, for the psychologically informed mediator, it may be a matter of degree. The issue of bullying and causing interruptions has been considered in the previous chapter. Where one spouse in a joint session acts in an overbearing and aggressive manner, preventing the other from being heard, the mediator may need to analyse with that spouse or party the reasons for such behaviour before intervening in any authoritarian manner. There may be a difference between a spouse expressing strong emotions while striving for control of the situation through a display of power, and one who is so manipulative as to render the other incapable of having a voice.

While not being obliged to ensure a 'just' settlement, where a proposed settlement has the semblance of injustice in the eyes of the mediator, it may be perfectly appropriate for the mediator to test the party's understanding of it. 'The offer you are proposing to accept may appear very unfair or one-sided to others looking at it. What do you feel about that?' Such an intervention may be equally appropriate if made to the offeror as to the offeree, for it may not be to the offeror's advantage to appear to be exploiting a weaker party. But if both parties are content – and here there is the advantage of intervals between sessions so that further advice can be sought – it would not be proper for the mediator to interfere by suggesting a different course of action. The ultimate mantra of the mediator will here be of great assistance: 'I am not here as a judge, but merely as a facilitator.'

The family mediator will not lose sight of the fact that mediation is as much about enabling relationships to end without rancour and bitterness as it is about restoring relationships. This can be achieved through the creation of mutual understandings and by dispelling misperception and assumptions. The mediator performs a valuable function simply by facilitating a dialogue between spouses who have lost the ability to communicate effectively – or at all.

Employment and Workplace Mediation

The distinction between employment and workplace mediation is often related to whether the employment relationship is to be restored or terminated. Employment mediation is said to govern those disputes where the relationship between employer and employee has terminated or is under consideration for termination. In workplace mediation, the principal objective is to restore and preserve the employee's relationship – whether with a fellow employee or with the employer. Nevertheless, for the purposes of considering the psychological aspects of both types of dispute, the distinction is more blurred and of less significance. Where a workplace dispute is not resolved, it will almost inevitably lead to a termination of the relationship, and may end up in litigation in the employment tribunal. Similarly, an employment dispute may be settled in mediation by the restoration of the relationship through reinstatement of the employee. Employment disputes tend to be more formal in nature, often with lawyers closely involved, and may be more regulated in terms of Employment Acts, and the ACAS

Codes. Workplace disputes are often less formal, with friends and colleagues more likely to be in attendance than lawyers.

Both employment and workplace conflicts involve the work environment and people's capacity to earn a living or to make a profit. As with many disputes, they deplete the parties of time, energy, productivity and money. Even the smallest quarrel in the workplace can have a ripple effect, with discomfort and loss of morale and productivity affecting a wider circle of people. The most minor irritation can snowball, resulting in polarization, with groups of people aligning themselves with one or other party. Workplace disputes will often revolve around complaints of discourtesy, perceived rudeness, bullying, or other elements of unacceptable behaviour. Tidiness, punctuality, loyalty may be seen as 'minor' complaints, yet they will be felt as having considerable weight and gravity by the complainant. Other disputes that may stray across the workplace and employment divide are: allocation of work or working hours; perceived insensitivity to disability issues; failure to 'deal appropriately' with fellow employees; performance and assessment issues; harassment and discrimination – these are all matters which may require psychologically informed management in order to avoid serious escalation. The ultimate concern is that if the dispute is left unresolved, the disgruntled employee may have a claim for constructive dismissal, whereby the employee claims that he or she was obliged to terminate the employment because of the conduct of the employer.

A meaningful difference between mediation in employment and workplace disputes on the one hand and mediation in other sectors on the other is the manner in which the mediator is appointed. In commercial and family disputes, it is the parties themselves who are likely to propose mediation and agree upon the mediator. In workplace and some employment cases, it is invariably the employer who proposes mediation to the other party or parties, and can select and sometimes impose the mediator, very often without any consultation with the parties. This may raise challenges for the mediator, for mediation is intended to be a voluntary process and so is generally considered preferable when it is entered into consensually. There will, however, always be a disparity between the parties, in any sector, in the level of 'eagerness' to mediate; the mediator must be ready to manage such varying levels of commitment, reluctance and scepticism.

However, in employment and workplace disputes, there may be a greater perception of compulsion. Even where the employer has done little more than *propose* mediation, it may nevertheless be perceived by one or other of the employees as the employer *imposing* mediation – and the mediator – upon the parties. In many cases, the employee may be steadfastly set against any idea of mediation, believing either that the parties are irreconcilable, or, alternatively, that the employer ought to have taken action earlier. The situation may be still further exacerbated by the mediator being an HR executive or some other staff member of the employer organization: here the perception of bias and absence of neutrality will inevitably be more acute.

These are all situations where empathy, non-judgmental acceptance, an awareness of the employee's and employer's self-esteem and value systems will all serve the mediator well. Similar considerations will apply in issues surrounding the choice of venue, the number of pre-mediation meetings held and who is asked to speak first at joint sessions.

Two further concerns arise for the mediator in relation to his or her neutrality in employment and workplace mediations. The first is that the mediator will invariably receive a report in advance from the employer setting out the nature of the dispute or problem, together with an outline of the issues that the mediator is requested to resolve. It may also include some opinion of a judgmental nature as to the parties involved. This information is likely to be unavoidably biased to some degree: it would be unrealistic to expect the employer to have *no* opinion, however much they may protest their utter impartiality and detachment. The mediator will bear in mind that any such express or implied opinion is the result of perceptions and assumptions; and that these are to be strictly bracketed by the mediator if he or she wishes to retain the impression of balanced independence. The mediator will also be sensitive to the existential proposition that it is wholly impossible to be *completely* objective, and so it may be equally impossible to maintain and demonstrate objectivity throughout. This will require greater and sustained effort in protecting the trust that the mediator is seeking to create.

The second area where the mediator's neutrality might be placed under scrutiny is in the joint session. It is common for mediators in the workplace model of mediation, as in the traditional family mediation model, to summarize the position of each party in the presence of the other. The risks associated with such a procedure have already been considered in relation to family mediation. They apply equally in both models of mediation: the parties in a workplace and employment dispute will have precisely the same desire to 'get the mediator on their side', and each will be hoping for vindication and the support of the mediator. So any conduct on the part of the mediator that gives rise to a risk of losing neutrality must be approached with caution.

The Employer as a Party to the Mediation

A further strain upon a mediator's ethical position of independence is the employer's request for a report about the mediation. It is understandable that a wise and benevolent employer will wish to learn from the mediator what it was that may have caused or contributed to the workplace dispute. They will have a commendable desire to learn from past mistakes so as to avoid future potential problems; this is particularly so where the relationship has been restored and the employer would benefit from a report in order better to monitor the future conduct of the parties. However, this may be impossible without breaching confidentiality. The prudent mediator might anticipate such a pitfall at an early stage, and so perhaps fully explain to the employer the position relating to confidentiality prior to the commencement of the mediation. Alternatively the mediator may obtain an agreement between the parties as to what is or is not to be reported back.

In many instances, it may be wise to consider the attendance of the employer as a party at the mediation. If it is clear from the outset that the employer has a positive interest, not only in the outcome of the dispute between two work colleagues, but also in the lessons to be learned from it, the mediator may consider with all concerned whether it would be of benefit to have the employer present as a party. This would avoid some of the difficulties surrounding confidentiality just mentioned. Further, it is not uncommon for the employer to be regarded by one or more of the parties as being to some extent culpable. Take, for example, a case of harassment: a party who sees himself or herself as the victim of such conduct frequently places some, if not equal, blame upon the employer, either in condoning the harassment or in failing to take timely and appropriate measures to address the problem. In these circumstances, it may be imperative for the mediator, with the consent of all parties, to propose or invite the employer to take part.

Finally, the mediator may have an important role in guiding the parties in a workplace mediation in formulating the settlement agreement, if there is one. This will be particularly critical where measures are to be put in place for the future. It is more straightforward when such agreements are confined to resolving issues in the past, for it is readily practical to tie up all loose ends. When, however, the agreement looks into the future, there may be endless possibilities for the accord to unravel. Here the mediator will need to anticipate potential problems that may arise and consider what, if anything, might need to be put in place to deal with them if and when they occur. In employment cases, where an employee may be giving up any statutory rights, a more formal and legally oriented agreement will be required; here the assistance and contribution of lawyers may be essential.

Community Mediation

The term 'community mediation' encompasses a broad spectrum of mediation models, ranging from the minor neighbour dispute through to complex multi-party international environmental issues. The term will also encompass inter-faith mediation between religious communities, inter-generational conflicts, restorative justice in victim/offender mediation, peer mediation in schools and gang mediation on the streets. Each will present its own peculiar psychological challenges, and some of these are now considered below.

Neighbour Disputes

Disputes between neighbours can be intensely disagreeable. Issues surrounding the home create powerful emotions: 'The Englishman's home is his castle.' Home occupiers, whether as owners or tenants, are particularly sensitive to disturbances of any kind, be they of noise, untidiness, unpleasant behaviour, or encroachments into territory. Land and bricks-and-mortar-type property often represent two levels of value: on an emotional level it may be the home where the parties and possibly their parents or children have lived, whether for lengthy or short periods; and it may also represent the home that they wish to pass on to their offspring. This has strong emotional overtones. On a more commercial level, it represents an asset with significant monetary value: a substantial investment for the future. These values, layered on top of each other, produce intense passions. Whether the property is owned or rented, disputes with neighbours can severely blight their daily lives: it is the home they leave in the morning to go to work, and the home to which they return after a full day's exertion and effort. To have this precious environment infected and encased in bitter wrangling is demeaning and demoralizing.

Yet neighbour disputes abound and are often lengthy and intractable. The cases are often referred to the mediator by a referral agency such as the police, or local councils, or a housing association; and the work of the mediator is often conducted in the most testing and demanding of atmospheres. The venue for such mediations is generally in the parties' own homes, with the mediators often obliged to mediate in small rooms (kitchens or lounges), where the television remains switched on and where children and pets are permitted to intervene at will. The mediators normally co-mediate, working in pairs at all times, and they shuttle, usually only once but often on several occasions, between the two properties over a period of days or weeks. Even before arrival at a party's home, the task of setting up the process and arranging mutually convenient times to visit can be problematic and highly frustrating for the mediators. They will be confronted with varying levels of emotion, ranging from distrust, scepticism and disinterest to ardent, passionate and obsessive sentiments. Parties will often be cynical as to the value of the process, or the prospects of success. Nor has the mediator the luxury of 'playing the commercial card': there is rarely a commercial incentive to resolve such disputes; rather, the disputes and the animosity have become such a part of the everyday lives of the neighbouring parties that they might be disoriented and unsettled were they to come to an end.

All these factors constitute severe tests for the mediator's skills, and it is perhaps surprising that, in the light of all the foregoing, neighbourhood community mediators are nearly always unpaid volunteers. But it is here that, once again, any psychotherapeutic knowledge comes to the mediator's aid. Understanding the parties' values as their source of the emotions, and recognizing the coping mechanisms that the parties adopt to restore and protect their self-esteem, will enable the mediator to navigate through these immensely difficult conflicts.

Community Environmental Disputes

Environmental issues affect an increasing number of communities. The management of natural resources comes into conflict with environmental policies, which in turn adversely affect the economic livelihoods and the interests and traditions of the members of the community. Foreign and national companies are seen to encroach upon land and property in order to exploit natural resources – to the detriment of local inhabitants. Oil-drilling activities, mining operations, fracking processes, the erection of mobile phone masts – all are resented and feared, and often perceived as the source of a multitude of ills befalling a local community. Symptoms ranging from minor headaches to foetal miscarriages and cancerous growths are commonly attributed to these environmental incursions. These disputes can therefore involve multiple parties, with a plethora of issues and a large number of divergent interests. The complexity of these disputes is exacerbated by the fact that the issues are inevitably controversial. This is aptly described by Steven Daniels and Gregg Walker, professors at the University of Oregon, in their research paper 'Lessons from the Trenches: Twenty Years of Using Systems Thinking in Natural Resource Conflict Situations' (2012):

> The controversial nature of these situations emerges in several dimensions. Firstly, many different view-points exist concerning

the various issues in the situation. Interest groups tend to form to promote narrow agendas, without a strong incentive to engage other groups or embed other issues in their advocacy. Second, tension or incompatibility in the situation may relate to one or more of the following: facts, culture, values, jurisdiction, history, personality, relationship and procedure. Third, parties may hold strong emotional ties to the issues and the landscape, including strong attachments to the place. Finally parties may display cognitive biases such as overconfidence.... that contribute to competitive frames.

The interest groups referred to in the above passage are likely to be the result of polarization, and the aligning behind them of like-minded individuals. Each group of stakeholders in the conflict will have a strong need to be heard, but, furthermore, will consist of individuals who have their own separate and distinct issues, and who also each have a similar desire to be heard. They will believe that their own issue is of the greatest importance and deserves prominence, and they will be indifferent and unsympathetic to the views of others, both within their own group and in other factions. Their views will have been formed on the basis of a broad range of disparate information, and their perceptions and assumptions will similarly diverge widely. They will be subject to NIMBY (Not In My Back Yard) attitudes and similar irrational biases, but each will hold their own subjective view and their subjective approach to be the only *objective* truth, thereby once again illustrating Kierkegaard's proposition (see Chapter 1). This inevitably creates emotional blocks to conversations and other attempts at communication. In these circumstances, the mediator faces a huge task. He or she will have the aim of securing greater mutual understandings, dispelling an overload of misperceptions and wrongful assumptions, and ultimately achieving a level of collaboration which may lead to shared evaluations and joint decision-making – all in an intensely volatile and hostile environment.

This will require a great deal more careful and diligent planning than a commercial or family dispute. The format will need to be permutational, while at the same time having a strong formulaic system at its base. In the 1990's, Daniels and Walker developed a systems-based facilitation methodology known as 'Collaborative Learning', which 'combined systems thinking and public policy negotiation' (Daniels and Walker, 2012). This, together with their use of 'systems diagramming', addresses the complexities, controversies and uncertainties entailed by these disputes, and constructs a shared understanding that, they say, 'help the public achieve their goals because it creates a means for them to expand the conversation beyond a merely agency-centric formulation' (Daniels and Walker, 2012).

Restorative Justice

When mediating between a victim of crime and the offender, the mediator will be confronted by what should be a seemingly familiar assembly of existential givens in both parties. However, despite the presence of these many common traits, a particular set of skills and special training for this model of conflict resolution is required. A mediator might be forgiven for believing that, because restorative justice is simply a process of facilitation – facilitating a dialogue between the two parties, albeit one is a victim of crime and the other a criminal – and therefore any mediator can perform that role. Indeed, there may be an image among the public that restorative justice simply involves a police officer sitting at a table with the victim and the offender, and saying to the offender: 'Come on, lad, say sorry to the lady and tell her why you stole her handbag.' The aim of the process is to repair the harm done by the offence, and an untrained mediator might exacerbate the harm already inflicted – possibly upon both the victim and the perpetrator.

Victims of crime invariably ask the same questions: 'Why did it happen?', 'Why me?' Until the offender furnishes these answers, the victim can only speculate and is left in an uncomfortable and uncertain state – in an already uncertain world. That uncertainty is exacerbated by another question: 'Will it happen again?' The offender is also, paradoxically, left with a sense of injustice, for the punishment meted out in the criminal justice system will almost always appear to the offender as excessively harsh and inappropriate. The perpetrator achieves no insight or understanding into the consequences of the criminal behaviour and is given little or no opportunity to make up for the harm done.

In many developing and emergent states in central and eastern Europe, victim-offender mediation was the first model of conflict resolution to be adopted, prior to that of commercial mediation. The reasons may be twofold: the Penal Code in these countries often permits the court to impose financial retribution or compensation; hence the proceedings take on more of a civil litigation and personal injury aspect; and secondly, issues of honour (as, for example, the infamous Albanian blood feud), frequently result in a continuation of the conflict, even long after the offender has served a prison sentence. Such perpetuation is often carried out by persons far removed from the original parties, both in terms of generational relationship or in contextual proximity. The sons, grandsons and other distant relatives are expected to take up arms to purge the offense. This has a particularly destabilizing effect upon small communities. Victim-offender mediation addresses the psychological needs of both parties, and serves to dissipate the emotional drivers that prolong the dispute.

Many of the skills deployed by the mediator will be identical to those used in other models of mediation, except that the emphases and priorities may differ. Creating a safe, non-judgmental environment that enables both parties to feel properly heard is paramount. There are many instances when a joint meeting is deemed inappropriate, even on occasions when both parties would be content – where, for example, each has wholly unrealistic expectations of the outcome. In these circumstances the mediator facilitates communication in other less direct ways. Nevertheless, the general purpose of the process is to facilitate more direct communication between the parties. In seeking to avoid further harm being inflicted upon either party, the mediator will need to be particularly sensitive to the emotions and dynamics in the room: for joint meetings are likely to be more fraught than in a commercial mediation. The mediator will therefore need to ensure that the time is right for a joint meeting; and so, if the joint meeting is to take place at all, it will have been preceded by several private and confidential sessions, to ensure that both parties are ready and adequately prepared.

The issues surrounding seating, the order in which parties are asked to speak problems of maintaining neutrality and impartiality, the need to bracket biases and assumptions – all these aspects have been considered in previous chapters and will apply equally in a joint session between victim and offender. The question of ground rules has also already been considered (see Chapter 8), but in order to ensure that both parties feel properly heard, careful thought will need to be given to the nature and extent of the ground rules, if any, that might be set in relation to interruptions and other potentially disruptive behaviour. Each party will need to have explained to them in a comprehensive manner precisely what is envisaged by the mediator in terms of conduct that will or will not be tolerated. Equally, the mediator will have considered with each party their respective assumptions about the aims and objectives of the process, together with their sensitivities as to the anticipated outcomes they hope to achieve.

10

The Future of Psychology in Dispute Resolution

In the late 1990's when the Mediation Skills course was launched at Regent's University London (then Regent's College), many people were hostile to the concept of introducing psychology to mediation and conflict resolution. The sceptics were doubtful as to its uses and benefits, and the cynics believed the approach to be unduly soft: too 'touchy-feely', 'fluffy' and lacking in commercial methodology. More recently, a very substantial majority of those involved in dealing with conflict have come to realize that a certain level of understanding of the human condition is essential in order to be effective in assisting parties to reach a resolution of their disputes. With the future passage of years, it may be that mediators will be permitted to mediate only after demonstrating some knowledge, training or experience in the psychological aspects of conflict.

Promoting Mediation

One of the prime areas for the need of some psychology in the future will be in the promotion of mediation as a universal and mainstream form of dispute resolution. The reluctance to mediate on the part of those in dispute and the inexorable attraction of litigation has been considered earlier (Chapter 8). It remains a worldwide conundrum that mediation has not been taken up in the manner and in the numbers that many believe it should. This enigma was described by this author in an article, 'Compulsory Mediation?', published in the *New Law Journal* in April 2010:

> Imagine for a moment that Mediation is a product – a stain remover – that can be purchased from any supermarket. Almost all who have used it praise it highly. The product 'does what it says on the tin': it is cheap, quick, is easy to use, and saves time, cost and energy. On the adjacent shelf is another stain remover called Litigation. Almost all who have used it are highly critical of it: it frequently fails to deliver its promise of success: it is extremely slow and difficult to use, leaves an unpleasant odour behind, and takes up huge amounts of time, money and energy. Yet people queue up to purchase Litigation, and leave Mediation on the shelf. Why?
>
> (2010: 499)

The paradox is universal. In virtually every jurisdiction around the globe, similar sentiments are voiced by a wide variety of practitioners: 'Why is mediation not universally embraced?' Yet most governments throughout all the five continents acknowledge that protracted litigation is a destructive and damaging element for society. It destroys businesses by depleting management of the three essential commodities: time, money and energy. By causing businesses to collapse, it harms family life and in turn adversely affects health and wellbeing. Ultimately, this has a detrimental effect upon the entire economy, whether through the reduction in productivity or by the additional burden placed upon the Health Service. Ever since the Woolf Reforms, published in Lord Woolf's Access to Justice Report as long ago as 1996, and the Lord Chancellor's Discussion Paper on Alternative Dispute Resolution in 1999, the government and the judiciary have sought to make litigation a matter of last resort. Reforms to Legal Aid, Sir Rupert Jackson's report on English Civil Litigation and the ensuing Costs reforms, MIAMs (Mediation Information and Assessment Meetings) in Family cases – all these initiatives have sought to persuade the litigant to move away from the courts and towards mediation. On each occasion, mediators have woken to a new dawn, hoping that the fresh measures and reforms might see the long-awaited increase in the take-up of mediation. On each occasion, the mediation community has been disappointed.

The Courts, from the Court of Appeal down to the District Judges courts, have all contributed in the push towards mediation. In numerous judgments and decisions, the use of mediation has been advocated and actively encouraged, and the failure to make use of it has been severely criticised. The courts have regularly imposed costs penalties upon parties who refuse unreasonably to enter into the mediation process, and the grounds upon which a party may be deemed reasonably to have refused mediation have been severely narrowed.

Thus the encouragement to mediate has become increasingly robust, and the proximity to a form of compulsion has rarely been greater. Is compulsory mediation the answer? This is not the appropriate place to debate the pros and cons of compulsory mediation: many column inches have already been devoted to the topic. However, while the concept of mandatory or compulsory mediation remains a matter of repugnance both to the government and to the purist mediator, the term 'Automatic Referral to Mediation' may be a better and more palatable phrase to use. Many, including this author, have nevertheless and for some time argued that, until an element of compulsion is introduced to oblige those in dispute to enter into mediation, it will remain a less attractive and a less significant form of alternative dispute resolution. It may even wither on the vine altogether. The psychology of the litigant, and the attraction to the human condition of a fight with the promise of victory, is such as to militate against the universal acceptance of mediation. It will always be a counter-intuitive process, and will inevitably constitute a less appealing model for resolving disputes to most ardent litigators. There are nevertheless those who believe that compulsion is anathema and counter-productive to mediation, and that the slow, drip-feed progress of mediation over the past 50 years will continue into the future. The debate will no doubt rage on. What is clear, however, is that a good degree of psychological analysis will need to be applied to the promotion and marketing of mediation if it is to prosper within a resistant public. More careful consideration needs to be given to the way mediation is sold to the public. The traditional methods of trumpeting its speed, its low cost and its high success rates have not been successful: parties in the heat of conflict have little concern about the length of time it will take, nor any fear as to the amount of money needed to be thrown at the dispute.

The psychological needs of parties in conflict must in future to be better addressed and more adequately met.

Online Dispute Resolution (ODR)

With the enormous advances in technology, does the future of mediation lie in online dispute resolution? It has already been proposed that, as conflict always involves people, it will eternally be personal. Yet, will the process eventually become so fully automated as to render the involvement of human beings virtually superfluous? If so, will there be any need for expertise in the psychology of human interaction?

In the foreword to the Report of the Civil Justice Council (CJC) on ODR, published in February 2015, the Rt Hon Lord Dyson, Chairman of the CJC and Master of the Rolls, stated:

There is no doubt that online dispute resolution (ODR) is an area with enormous potential for meeting the needs of the [Civil Justice] system and its users in the 21st Century. Its aim is to broaden access to justice and resolve disputes more easily, quickly and cheaply. The challenge lies in delivering a system that fulfils that objective ... At a time of major pressure on public spending and high legal costs, ODR offers a major opportunity to help many people for whom public funding to resolve disputes is not available, or for whom legal costs are prohibitive. ODR is also in harmony with wider changes in society, in particular the advances in technology and the large scale use of online services to transact all forms of business.

The Report examined the potential of online dispute resolution for Small Claims civil disputes (where the value is less than £25,000), but it is thought that it might be extended to family disputes and other similar tribunal cases. The Report further envisaged a variety of techniques under the term ODR, whereby traditional courtrooms are avoided, and disputes are settled online. The involvement of human beings in some ODR platforms will remain significant, where, for example, facilities may be provided for judges, mediators, or negotiators to handle disputes, while communicating electronically. In other models little or no human intervention will be required. Thus the ODR platforms range from online fully automated transactions, such as 'blind bidding', to the highly sophisticated 'virtual mediation rooms'. The technology underpinning ODR is evolving rapidly, and the advances being made are in many respects astounding. For example, computer programs are available and are being further developed, whereby the mood and emotional state of the person typing on the computer keyboard can be identified, analysed and revealed.

From a psychological perspective, however, it remains appropriate constantly to bear in mind that, whatever the level of technology, a dispute can never exist without human involvement. Those who use ODR will share the existential givens of emotions, self-esteem and values, and will unavoidably be confronted by uncertainty, temporality and transiency. These and other psychological attributes will govern whatever data they input to the computer; and the manner in which the data is received and analysed will always be exposed to subjective interpretation by the other party.

Training in Mediation and Conflict Resolution

Mediation-training organizations are frequently castigated for churning out accredited mediators into an already saturated market. Yet the mediation skills taught are skills for life. Whether or not the graduates from these courses ultimately become active mediators, they will have acquired conflict-handling skills which will be invaluable in any sector, industry, profession or employment. They will have learned the techniques of dealing with emotions; gained an insight into assuaging anger; acquired an understanding of the motivations and behavioural strategies of people in conflict; and will have increased their level of self-awareness about themselves. It is therefore suggested that those who train mediators need not feel chastised: they are creating more rounded and civilized personalities in the community.

Academic Training in Mediation

There is likely to be an increasing tendency towards academic appreciation of mediation skills. Many still question the feasibility of training a mediator in the space of approximately 40 hours, irrespective of the intensity of the training. They contend that a much greater academic underpinning of the 'accreditation' is likely to be required. 'If mediation is to become a respected profession, mediators will need to be respected.' This is the understandable mantra of many in the mediation fraternity. Postgraduate courses are evolving; advanced mediation training may become the norm.

Mediation may constitute a compulsory module in many law courses both at undergraduate and postgraduate level.

Negotiation will always remain a natural and necessary part of any dispute resolution process. Sir Rupert Jackson's report on English Civil Litigation (2010) encouraged the use of negotiation in the early stages of a dispute, and the emphasis on proportionality in litigation will ensure that negotiation continues to play a significant role in all ADR models and processes. There is a consequent need to ensure that a more empathic style of negotiation continues to be taught – as it is on mediation courses. There may be a trend in the training of professional vocational courses for barristers and solicitors to teach more *interest-based* negotiation skills. The Bar Professional Training Course (BPTC), which superseded the Bar Vocational Course (BVC) in 2010–11, places increased emphasis on principled and empathic styles of negotiation. Similarly, the Professional Skills Course for Solicitors, pursuant to the SRA (Solicitors Regulation Authority) Training Regulations 2014, includes such 'softer' negotiation skills as a core activity in the training.

Mediation training in schools (Peer Mediation) is a growth area. Mediation *by* young pupils and students *for* young pupils and students is thought to be a pathway to the future of conflict-resolution processes. Pupils undergoing such training exhibit natural skills that adult trainees find problematic. They do not carry the same conditioned psychological baggage as do more seasoned world travellers. Yet the conscious influence of existentialist psychologies is unlikely to be present in any significant form, and hence it is not addressed here.

Varying Styles of Mediation

As well as the existence of differing models of mediation (such as commercial, family, employment and others), there is also a diversity of *styles* of mediation, as, for example, facilitative, evaluative, transformative and narrative styles. The respective benefits and effectiveness of evaluative and facilitative styles of mediation has previously been considered by Strasser and Randolph (2004: 66); nevertheless, the debate will undoubtedly continue. The former style is more 'directive and interventionist' whereby the mediator provides the parties with an 'evaluation' of the respective strengths and weaknesses of parties' cases. The latter is said to be confined to assisting the parties to communicate and interact with each other in a more collaborative fashion.

It is also worth mentioning two further styles of mediation: narrative and transformative. Narrative mediation is based upon narrative therapy, involving 'story-telling'. It was largely promoted by two New Zealand therapists, John Winslade and Gerald Monk, leading lights in the narrative therapy movement of the 1990's. This approach seeks to promote a deeper understanding of the dispute through the context of the story, and the party's role in it. Transformative mediation was introduced to the world in *The Promise of Mediation* by Baruch Bush and Folger (1994). This style of mediation stresses the importance of 'empowerment and recognition', and focuses more upon the process than the outcome of mediation.

It is respectfully suggested that there may be little benefit in seeking to analyse which specific style is more appropriate for any particular type of dispute: a good mediator may pass seamlessly through each of these styles of mediation during the course of a single day's mediation. The mediator, for example, may commence in narrative mode, hearing the party's account as a form of story in which the mediator can intervene. The mediator may then progress through to a more facilitative mode, becoming a follower rather than a leader, and simply easing and assisting the communication and negotiation between the parties. By achieving a better understanding between the parties, the mediator may thereby have entered into a 'transformative' model, precipitating a transformation in the relationship between the parties as well as in their understanding of themselves. If the mediator feels that a trusting relationship has been created and there is a powerful rapport, it may then be appropriate to begin challenging and reality-testing – in effect, becoming more evaluative. This author would contend that any form of challenge or reality test must by its very nature be 'evaluative', for it proceeds from the basis of a norm postulated by the mediator. The 'reality' will inevitably be that of the mediator, and the party's expressed position will thus be challenged and tested against the 'evaluated' opinion of the mediator. As has repeatedly been proposed in previous chapters, there is no such phenomenon as *objective* reality.

Cross-Border and Trans-Cultural Mediation

The increased globalization of conflict has been brought about by a process of international integration, resulting from a worldwide exchange of views, concepts, ideas and cultures. Advances in transportation, telecommunications and internet have increased the cross-fertilization of economic and cultural activities, and have resulted in a further eroding of the significance of national borders. A greater number of international conflicts are being resolved through cross-border mediation.

There is an instinctive perception that people of different nationalities are very 'different': that they will respond and react very differently to similar situations. Yet existentialist philosophy teaches us otherwise. As Bernard Mayer put it in *The Dynamics of Conflict*:

> In fact, human beings across a wide range of cultures exhibit similar emotional responses. If people are insulted or attacked, they respond with anger or fear. If they experience a major loss, they grieve. If they accomplish something very important to them, they rejoice. For all practical purposes, people from different cultures experience the same range of emotions in conflict, and for conflict to be dealt with, mechanisms for the release and validation of feelings are necessary.
>
> (2012: 100)

The above passage encapsulates many of the existentialist concepts discussed in earlier chapters: it in effect describes the coping mechanisms that are adopted globally, in order to deal with the universally shared givens such as emotions, self-esteem and values. Many of the variations noted in differing cultures are simply variations of values and value systems. Diverse ethnic and cultural groups will prioritize certain values in different ways. Thus, honour and face will be dominant in one culture and absent in another. What is regarded as disrespectful in one culture will be the norm or meaningless and uncontroversial in another. Many of these values will have bases in historical, religious, or ethnic experiences.

From a psychological perspective, therefore, it is often counter-productive to be overly sensitive to differing cultures and norms. It may be impossible to avoid entirely the pitfalls of innocently and unintentionally violating the customs and values of another. Obsessively seeking to avoid such transgressions may appear patronizing. The psychologically informed mediator, versed in existentialist concepts, will appreciate the need to understand only the shared givens – the remainder are mere variations upon a theme. Thus sensitivity to the dynamics of interpersonal relationships, being open-minded, having regard to a range of differing values, being aware of the self-esteem of those around us, and appreciating the need to be heard – all these qualities will enable the mediator to enjoy working across borders and with a diversity of cultures.

Regulation

Finally, it is necessary to turn to the knotty problem of regulation. Some will argue that the public has no real desire for the regulation of mediators. The concern of the average litigant, as we have seen, is not to find an experienced and successful mediator, but to select one who is most likely to vindicate the litigant's position and to 'find in the litigant's favour'. Issues as to quality assurance in relation to the mediator seem often to pale into insignificance in comparison with the desire for vindication. Quality assurance for the public users of mediation, however, is an important issue for mediators if they wish to be seen as a respectable and competent profession.

Although there is no governmental regulation of mediation or of mediators, the Civil Mediation Council (CMC) seeks to be 'the voice of mediation', and to be recognized as the leading authority in the UK for all matters related to civil, commercial, workplace and other non-family mediation. The CMC introduced a system of individual registration of mediators, and the contact details of the registered mediators can be accessed by visiting the CMC website. Such registration schemes may constitute an element of 'light touch' regulation. The Ministry of Justice similarly has a list of CMC Accredited Mediation Provider Panels on its website, and the contact details for each Provider Panel are set out there and are searchable in geographical order. Most of the Ministry of Justice-approved Mediation Provider Panels are also listed on the website of the National Mediation Providers Association (NMPA). Most organizations who provide mediation training will have a list of their alumni who are accredited mediators, including Regent's University London.

A European Code of Conduct for Mediators (2004) was developed in collaboration with the European Commission and launched in Brussels in July 2004. It was linguistically revised in July 2009. Adherence to the Code is entirely voluntary, although many mediation organizations in the UK have committed themselves and their members to respecting the Code. It is generally regarded as a fairly bland document, dealing only very generally with issues of independence and impartiality, the fairness of the process and confidentiality.

It is questionable as to what extent all of the above will be of assistance to the member of the public looking for a mediator. It will not provide a guarantee that the party will be able to engage in a trusting relationship with the mediator, nor that there will be instant rapport. The astute potential disputant will perhaps appreciate the need for a psychologically informed mediator, who may be able more effectively to guide them through the emotional minefield of human behaviour in conflict.

Bibliography

Aho, K. (2014), *Existentialism: An Introduction*. Cambridge: Polity Press.

Aubrey-Johnson K., with Curtis, H. (2012), *Making Mediation Work for You*. London: Legal Action Group.

Baruch Bush, R. A. and Folger, J.P. (1994), *The Promise of Mediation*. San Francisco: Jossey-Bass.

Cialdini, R. (1984), *Influence: The Psychology of Persuasion*. New York: HarperCollins.

Civil Justice Council (2015) *Report on Online Dispute Resolution for Low Value Civil Claims*. London: CJC

Cloke, K. (2001), *Mediating Dangerously*. San Francisco: Jossey-Bass.

Coleman, D. (1995), *Emotional Intelligence*. London: Bloomsbury.

Cooper, M. (2003), *Existential Therapies*. London: Sage.

Craver, C. B. (2005), *Effective Legal Negotiation and Settlement*. Newark: LexisNexis Matthew Bender.

Daniels, S. E. and Walker, G. B. (2012), 'Lessons from the Trenches: Twenty Years of Using Systems Thinking in Natural Resource Conflict Situations'. *Systems Research and Behavioral Science*, 29 (March/April 2012), 104–115. John Wiley & Sons Wiley Online Library.

Deurzen-Smith, E. van (1988), *Existential Counselling in Practice*. London: Sage.

Deutsch, M., Coleman P. and Marcus E. (2006), *The Handbook of Conflict Resolution*. San Francisco: Jossey-Bass.

Dyer, W. (2009), *A New Way of Thinking, a New Way of Being: Experiencing the Tao Te Ching*. Carlsbad: Hay House.

Festinger, L., Riecken, H. and Schachter, S. (1956), *When Prophecy Fails*. Minneapolis: University of Minnesota Press.

Fisher R. and Ury, Y. (1981), *Getting to Yes*. London: Random House.

Frankl, V. (2004), *Man's Search for Meaning*. Reading: Rider.

Gandhi, M (1993), *An Autobiography: The Story of My Experiments with Truth*. Boston: Beacon Press.

Heidegger, M. (2001), *Zollicon Seminars* (trans. F. Mayr and R. Askay). Evanston: Northwestern University Press.

Iacovou, S. and Weixel-Dixon, K. (2015), *Existential Therapy*. East Sussex: Routledge.

Jackson, R. (2010), *Review of Civil Litigation Costs: Final Report*. Norwich: TSO (The Stationery Office).

Kaufman, K (ed.) (1989), *Existentialism from Dostoevsky to Sartre*, New York: Meridian Publishing Company, trans. P. Mairet).

Kierkegaard, S. (1844), *The Concept of Anxiety* (trans. W. Lowry). Princeton: Princeton University Press.

———(1844), *Fear and Trembling* (trans. A. Hannay). New York: Penguin Books

——— (1846), *Concluding Unscientific Postscript* (trans. D.F. Swenson) Princeton: Princeton University Press.

Lindsay, A. D. (trans.) (1719), *Plato: The Republic*. Sheridan: Heron Books by arrangement with J. M. Dent & Sons.

Macquarrie, J. (1972), *Existentialism: An Introduction, Guide and Assessment*. London: Penguin Books.

Mayer, B. (2012), *The Dynamics of Conflict*. San Francisco: Jossey-Bass.

Merleau-Ponty, M. (1945), *Phenomenology of Perception* (trans. C. Smith). New York: Routledge.

Randolph, P. (2010), 'Compulsory Mediation?', *New Law Journal*, Procedure and Practice.

Roberts, M. (1997), *Mediation In Family Disputes*. Farnham: Ashgate Publishing.

Russell, B. (1993), *The Conquest of Happiness*. Abingdon: Routledge Classics.

Sartre, J. P. (1956), *Being and Nothingness* (trans. H. E. Barnes). New York: Washington Square Press.

——— (1962), *Sketch for a Theory of Emotions*. London: Routledge.

Solomon, R. C. (2008). *Handbook of Emotions*. Guildford: Guildford Press.

Spinelli, E. (2005), *The Interpreted World*. London: Sage.

Strasser, F. (1999), *Emotions: Experiences in Existential Psychotherapy and Life*. London: Duckworth.

Strasser, F. and Randolph, P. (2004), *Mediation: A Psychological Insight into Conflict Resolution*. London: Continuum.

Strasser, F. and Strasser, A. (1997), *Existential Time-Limited Therapy*. Chichester: Wiley.

Warnock, M. (1970), *Existentialism*. New York: Oxford University Press.

Index

Locators in *italics* indicate a diagram.